T0130864

# SECRET
# **BOSTON**

*Kiernan P. Schmitt*

JONGLEZ PUBLISHING

Travel guides

**W**e immensely enjoyed writing the *Secret Boston – An unusual guide* and hope that, like us, you will continue to discover the unusual, secret, and lesser-known facets of this city.

Accompanying the description of some sites, you will find historical information and anecdotes that will let you understand the city in all its complexity.

*Secret Boston – An unusual guide* also sheds light on the numerous yet overlooked details of places we pass by every day. These details are an invitation to pay more attention to the urban landscape and, more generally, to regard our city with the same curiosity and attention we often feel when travelling ...

Comments on this guide and its contents, as well as information on sites not mentioned, are welcome and will help us to enrich future editions.

Don't hesitate to contact us:
Email: info@jonglezpublishing.com

N

Readi

93

Burlington

Bedford

Woburn　Stoneha

4

95

3

Lexington

Winchester

2

2

Arlington

Medfo

Belmont

Waltham

Somervil

20

Watertown

95

90

90

p. 86

Cambrid

Newton

Fenw

Brookline

9

9

Wellesley

135

Needham

WORCESTER

Dedham

109

138

0　　　　5　　　　10 km

95

PROVIDENCE

95

93

NEWBURYPORT, PORTSMOUTH ↑     GLOUCESTER ↑

95

1

95

Peabody

Salem

Wakefield

107

Marblehead

129

1

Swampscott

Saugus

Lynn

1

Melrose

107

1

Nahant

Malden

Everett

Revere

16

1

p. 12

Chelsea

Winthrop

*East Boston*

*North End*

**BOSTON**

✈ Logan International Airport

*ack ay*

*South Boston*

*South End*

p. 150

*Long Island*

Hull

*Peddocks Island*

93

1

Milton

28

Quincy

Hingham

Weymouth

Braintree

53

3

↓ NEW BEDFORD     → PLYMOUTH, CAPE COD

p. 248

*Atlantic Ocean*

# CONTENTS

## *Central Boston*

# *Cambridge*

# CONTENTS

## *Brookline, Fenway, Back Bay*

## *West*

## *East*

# Central Boston

# NORMAN B. LEVENTHAL MAP COLLECTION

*Priceless maps at a hotel bar*

*Boston Harbor Hotel*
*70 Rowes Wharf*
*Take a left past check-in toward the hotel restaurant*
*Red Line/South Station*

In 2007, at the age of 90, Boston native and renowned real estate developer Norman Leventhal made news by donating $10 million to the Boston Public Library – the single biggest gift the library had ever received. The money was earmarked to endow a center founded three years prior to educate and celebrate all things geographic: the Norman B. Leventhal Map Center.

Leventhal, who died in 2015, was an ardent lover of cartography and a collector of historic maps. His first acquisition was made in London in the 1970s and was, fittingly, a map of his hometown; Leventhal continued to seek out maps that showed the exploration, charting, and development of the city, its harbor, and the American Northeast.

Some 400 pieces from Leventhal's personal collection joined an archive of over 200,000 maps and atlases at today's Map Center, located at the main branch of the Boston Public Library.

The Center hosts rotating public exhibitions and allows access to its archives by appointment. However, there is a more comfortable way to take in these unique works of art: a subset of the Leventhal Map Collection hangs on the walls of the Boston Harbor Hotel just outside the hotel's bar.

Leventhal oversaw the construction of today's Rowes Wharf, a major public space and home to the luxury hotel, and deemed it fitting that travelers should learn about the history of Boston and its environs.

The hotel collection is laid out chronologically to take hotel guests from early European exploration in the 1500s through to settlement and development in the 19th and 20th century. There is a particular focus on the city's footprint at the time of the American Revolution.

So, with a gin and tonic or Scotch in hand, amid businesspeople wearily finishing PowerPoint presentations, take in these priceless antique documents. Be sure not to miss John Bonner's "The Town of Boston in New England" – the first printed map of the city – or John Calvin Smith's delightful 1845 "Map of the United States of America, Canada, and Texas," which features indigenous wildlife gallivanting along its busy borders.

# HIDDEN MERMAIDS MOSAIC

*Wet Working Women*

*South Station Headhouse at the corner of Summer Street
and Atlantic Avenue
Red Line/South Station*

In 2005, members of the Boston chapter of WTS – a professional organization dedicated to the advancement of women in the transportation industry – decided they wanted to give an artwork to the city in honor of the unsung contributions of female engineers, architects, public servants, and other professionals to the creation and day-to-day workings of the local transportation system.

In 2019, "NETWORK" was revealed – a 650 square foot glass mosaic map color-coded to identify roads (light gray), railroads (medium gray), and subways (dark gray). Boston's premier train depot, South Station, is represented with a golden dot.

But these transportation markers account for only a small portion of the whole: much of the surface is dedicated to a blue-green ocean, underlining Boston's connection to its harbor.

This large mosaic ocean can read like background noise to the thousands of commuters streaming by each day, a blur of calming color and nothing more. However, close observation reveals that hidden within the vastness of the ocean are three nearly indiscernible mermaids.

Even more surprising (and a bit bizarre), these are professional mermaids at work: each is handling complicated-looking surveying equipment.

What's going on here?

Ellen Harvey, the artist behind "NETWORK," provides this explanation: "As sea levels rise, vengeful mermaids start to survey the Boston transportation network. They are almost invisible, like the many underacknowledged female transportation professionals that WTS-Boston commissioned this piece to honor. Will we be caught in their net or will we (net)work together to escape our fate?"

Mermaids – so often the temptresses or one-note beauties in literature – are thus transformed into symbols of female empowerment and the dire consequences for coastal cities of ignoring climate change. It's a complicated message with a powerful punch – for those few who can actually make it out.

# SHOEPRINTS AT THE UNITED SHOE MACHINERY CORPORATION BUILDING

*A footwear cathedral*

*160 Federal Street*
*Red Line/South Station*

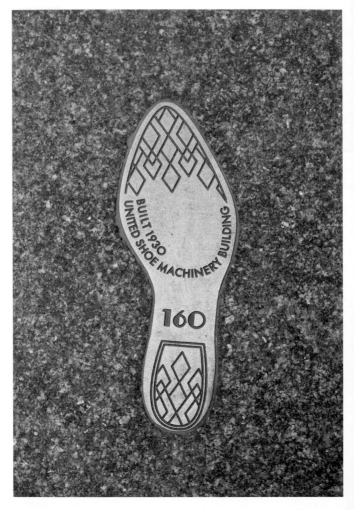

**B**oston is broadly regarded as a town built on academia. But the argument could be made that Massachusetts's capital city is secretly an industrial town – and the industry is shoemaking.

The state's history in footwear stretches back some way. The first American shoemakers set up shop in Salem in 1629. In 1750, a Welsh immigrant and master shoemaker named John Adam Dagyr established the first shoe manufacturing assembly line in Lynn, MA. In the 1800s, Massachusetts inventors modernized the industry with the introduction of sewing machines that could puncture leather, "pegging machines" to attach hard soles to the main body of the shoe, and "lasting machines" which made it possible to mechanically stretch leather and attach soles on foot molds.

Suddenly, shoes were big business, and huge Massachusetts-based corporations sprang up. Even today, Boston's skyline is dotted with the logos of many major shoe brands' HQs, including Puma, Converse, and New Balance.

This history is preserved in the form of an Art Deco skyscraper downtown, the former home of the United Shoe Machinery Corporation. USMC was formed through the merger of the three most powerful footwear manufacturing companies, which together held 70% of patents on shoe machinery. Shoemakers of the time couldn't own their equipment outright and had to rent machinery from USMC in order to do their work.

The company's imposing headquarters, completed in 1930, speaks to its monopolistic power: by 1929, USMC controlled 98% of the American shoe machinery business. Even the Great Depression hardly impacted the company's bottom line.

The 24-story ziggurat, which was saved by preservationists when plans for a new office tower were proposed, maintains its original character, with only a few clues to its origins. Several metal shoeprints, decorated with a natty diamond pattern, are inlaid in the sidewalk just outside its entrance. Above the address signage on its exterior sits a simple, remarkably boring shoe in metal relief.

## Don't overlook the cows

While much of the exterior metalwork is the standard fare of abstracted figures and floral patterns, don't overlook the cows. High up, in between trapezoidal vases, sit the visages of several unhappy-looking steers, a tribute to the leather that USMC used in so many of its shoes.

# BOSTON BRICKS

*History underfoot*

*Winthrop Lane*
*Red Line or Orange Line/Downtown Crossing*

In 1985, a hidden alley in central Boston was re-envisioned as a public art project – yet remains virtually unknown today. Squished between bustling commercial streets, Winthrop Lane is paved with bricks and 100 bronze brick-shaped reliefs sculpted and installed by artists Kate Burke and Gregg LeFevre.

The bronze sculptures each spotlight a moment in the history of the city, from the famous – the Boston Tea Party, Paul Revere's ride – to the wholly obscure – the first recorded use of a baseball mitt in 1875, the invention of the sewing machine in 1845, the first American post office opening in 1639.

The designs play with perspective and composition. Three Lilliputian rowers work away in their individual sculls and are presented in bird's-eye view, transforming the brick into a little outlet of the Charles River. A brick showing a fence with seven different finials memorializes the varieties of cast-iron decoration on the historic fences of the parks and cemeteries near Boston Common. The towers of the Longfellow Bridge are transformed into salt and pepper shakers.

Many are unexpectedly witty or intentionally confusing. Burke recounted her relationship with Boston: "I knew many inside jokes Bostonians knew and wanted to give students and tourists something to ponder. No matter the audience, the intention was that the bricks should be seen quickly or pondered to be understood later. I loved hearing stories of folks walking the Lane for months and having a brick inspire a burst of laughter after getting the joke."

A detailed, seemingly anatomically accurate fish challenges the viewer to identify it: "COD OR SCROD?" One brick simply provides a recipe for Boston baked beans.

Certain bricks are indecipherable to all but the truest Bostonians.

One could spend minutes studying the relief labeled "Combat Zone" before finally seeing a fishnet stocking-clad calf and a very high heel: the Combat Zone was a term used in the 1960s to refer to a rundown Boston neighborhood packed with adult bookstores, strip clubs, and other sordid businesses.

Other bricks simply list names. Burke explained, "This is now politically incorrect, but was once seen as a source of pride. I scoured the phone book for names to use. The crown of this group was the idea that everyone is Irish. O'Brian, O' Burke, O' Schmitt, O'Schwartz, O'Reilly, Oh'Really, Oh' Boy!"

# THE FLOATING HOSPITAL
# FOR CHILDREN PHOTO GALLERY

## *An experiment at sea*

*Tufts Medical Center*
*Use the main entrance; on Floor 3, turn left around a café and enter a bridge over*
*Washington Street*
*800 Washington Street, Boston*
*Orange Line/Tufts Medical Center*

Within Tufts, an obscure hallway has been converted into a makeshift photo gallery celebrating the history of the Floating Hospital, a nautical children's medical facility that trawled Boston Harbor for 33 years.

In 1894, a minister named Rufus Tobey and a group of civic-minded Bostonians bought a barge and converted it into a hospital for impoverished children. The group believed that the lack of fresh air in Boston's slums caused deadly childhood ailments, including cholera and whooping cough. The Harbor, with its restorative breezes, was to be the antidote to the city's smog and dirt.

In its early years, the Floating Hospital doubled as a party boat in the evenings; as soon as the sick children off-loaded, partiers would board for a night of dancing and music. In time, the Floating Hospital became a fully professional operation, with nurses residing on the boat full-time and physicians making regular rounds throughout the summer months.

In 1927, the ship burned. The fire was discovered by a policeman who was performing a nightly patrol of the North End neighborhood known as "Lover's Lane." According to the *Boston Globe*, Patrolman Michael Rizzo was "clearing the pier of 'spooners,'" when he spied a small flicker, which developed "at an almost incredible rate of speed" into flames 300 feet tall and viewable for miles. The fire occurred in the off-season, thus no patients or personnel were on board, though four crew members did abandon ship. Three got to a lifeboat, but fire forced the captain to jump out of his office window into the dark waters below.

While there were plans to build a new boat, a land-based facility proved more practical. Still, Tufts continued to call its children's facility the "Floating Hospital" up to 2020.

## The world's first synthetic milk: created on board

In time, the Floating Hospital expanded its services. In response to a cow and breast milk shortage, a milk lab opened, and, in 1919, Dr. Alfred Bosworth created the world's first synthetic milk, called "Similac," on board. An early ad touted that Similac was "a completely reconstructed milk in which all the elements of cow's milk have been rearranged to meet the physical, chemical, and medical requirements of a diet for infants." Similac went into commercial production and is still available today.

# ANCIENT FISHWEIR PROJECT

*Fish traps on dry land*

*Held yearly, usually in July*
*Latest at fishweir.org*
*Red Line or Green Line/Park Street for Boston Common event*

Boston Harbor Shore Line Circa 1630

Each year, artist Ross Miller oversees a public art installation on Boston Common which honors Massachusetts's Native American past through the construction of a fishweir – an elaborate four foot high wall made of brush and saplings woven through thousands of upright wooden stakes. The weir was a trap to catch migrating fish, though archeologists disagree about the size and permanence of the structures. Miller opts for a long, impressive version spanning the Common.

The Ancient Fishweir Project was inspired by the discovery of the remains of fishweirs in Boston's Back Bay neighborhood. In 1913 and 1939, subway and building construction efforts unearthed sharpened wooden stakes 28 to 40 feet below ground.

In the later discovery, observers estimated as many as 65,000 stakes were buried within a 3 acre area, suggesting a complex structure and likely a sizeable Native group attending to it. Later radiocarbon dating revealed excavated wood from the area ranged from 3,700 to 5,000 years old, far before modern landfill had buried the tidal bay that gives the neighborhood its name. The range of ages suggested that fishweirs may have been smaller and more routinely built by groups of people that migrated to the coast in the warmer seasons.

Since 2001, students from the Boston Public Schools have assisted in the creation of the Boston Common fishweir, and groups from Native American communities often join to perform and participate during the yearly celebration.

## NEARBY
## *"A Once and Future Shoreline" artwork*

A short walk from Green Line B C D E or Blue Line/Government Center nearby the Ancient Fishweir Project, Miller has created another provocative work that points to the way modern Boston has transformed its relationship with the sea. "A Once and Future Shoreline" is an easily overlooked artwork on the sidewalk of the plaza directly in front of Faneuil Hall (near the Sam Adams statue.) Miller has etched into the sidewalk beach detritus – seaweed, shells, egg casings, fish – to mark off the pre-Colonial shoreline. The work sharply nods to climate change's power to return the sea to where it once was.

In the same area, Miller has also etched dotted lines that reflect the land plots in the area from an 1820 map.

# HIDDEN POE ON SOLDIERS AND SAILORS MONUMENT

## *Literary hide-and-seek*

*Highest point in Boston Common*
*Tremont Street and Park Street*
*Red Line or Green Line/Park Street*

While many cities in the U.S. regard Edgar Allen Poe as a local hero, Boston and Poe have a more complex relationship. The creator of the detective genre and master of literary horror lived and worked in many north-east cities, including New York and Baltimore, but he was born on Carver Street in Boston. He famously despised the city and its insular educated elite.

In 1845, Poe wrote, "We like Boston. We were born there -- and perhaps it is just as well not to mention that we are heartily ashamed of the fact. The Bostonians are very well in their way. Their hotels are bad. Their pumpkin pies are delicious. Their poetry is not so good … But with all these good qualities the Bostonians have no soul. They have

always evinced towards us individually, the basest ingratitude for the services we rendered them … The Bostonians are well-bred – as very dull persons very generally are."

And thus Bostonians have long debated whether to embrace or reject Poe. In 2014 the decision was made to embrace: a life-size statue of Poe mid-stride was installed at the corner of Boylston, just off the Common.

However, in 2019, historian Kathryn Grover made a discovery: Poe had been hiding in plain sight for 142 years on the park's most prominent statue: the 1877 Soldiers and Sailors Monument, sculpted by Martin Milmore to remember those who died in the Civil War. Its four bas-reliefs are often overlooked. In one entitled "The Departure," a line of soldiers leaves for combat, marching in front of a row of VIPs. Grover unearthed a document from Milmore identifying the man furthest to the left, with his hand over his heart, as none other than Poe.

This is perplexing. Poe lived in Boston for only five months of his adult life, yet stands among well-known and respected members of the Boston elite. Plus, the scene is set in the 1860s: Poe died in 1849.

Why Milmore made the decision to include a dead Boston-hater is lost to time, a mystery befitting a tale by Poe.

# THE GREAT ELM PLAQUE

*A tree well-remembered*

*Boston Common*
*The plaque is just downhill from the Soldiers and Sailors Monument towards the eastern border of the park*
*Red Line or Green Line/Park Street*

New Englanders are known for their flintiness, but there is one former resident of Boston that, for centuries, seems to have brought out the poet in every true son of the city. It was a tree, popularly known as The Great Elm.

The Great Elm was revered as "Boston's Oldest Inhabitant." In his 1838 book *The Boston Common Or, Rural Walks in Cities*, Nehemiah Adams referred to it as our "vegetable patriarch." He went even further in 1842: "That tree is to antiquity with us what a pyramid is in Egypt. It is like the pillars of Hercules, bounding the unknown ages which preceded the arrival of the Pilgrims."

The myth surrounding the tree derived from its size, geography, and suspected age. The Great Elm was located in Boston Common, one of only three large trees shown on early maps. In 1855, it was believed to be 72 feet high. Its size led many to believe the tree pre-dated Europeans settlers' arrival in Massachusetts; a ring count later placed its planting somewhere in the 1630s.

For decades, the tree served civic purposes dark and light. It shaded cattle grazing in the Common (some imagine a young Ben Franklin climbing its branches when he should have been minding the family cow.) British Redcoats camped beneath it and the American Sons of Liberty gathered there. The tree was a meeting spot for daily chores and recreation. Some credit a 1790 sermon delivered by Reverend Jesse Lee beneath its boughs as the founding of Methodism in New England.

It was also the site of public hangings and duels. In 1659, Quakers William Robinson and Marmaduke Stevenson were hanged from its branches by Puritan leaders for heresy. Fellow Quaker Mary Dyer was hanged a year later. (A statue of Dyer now sits on the grounds of the State House looking down on the site of the Great Elm.)

Native Americans were likewise killed at the Great Elm, including Nipmuc leader Tantamous during King Philip's War (1675–1676) between the settlers and indigenous peoples.

No tree can last forever; a winter storm brought it down in February 1876. The populace was bereft and scrambled for mementos. An ornate chair made from its wood was donated to the Boston Public Library. The Massachusetts Historical Society (see p. 164) has in its collection a pair of wooden earrings crafted from remains of the Great Elm; fittingly, they are tiny Liberty Bells.

Today, just downhill from the Soldiers and Sailors Monument towards the eastern border of the park, a plaque commemorates the tree.

# ETHER MONUMENT

*Painkillers controversy*

Boston Public Garden near the corner of Arlington Street and Marlborough Street
Red Line or Green Line/Park Street

While the Boston Public Garden is most famous for its swan boats and shady benches, a towering monument in the northwest corner celebrates a medical innovation: the use of ether as anesthesia. At the nearby Massachusetts General Hospital, on October 16, 1846, a dentist named William T.G. Morton made history by administering ether to Gilbert Abbott, who was suffering from a vascular neck tumor. Surgeon John Collins Warren then cut out the tumor, with Abbott reporting no pain. You can still visit the operating theater, now dubbed "The Ether Dome" (see p. 34).

Credit for the discovery was later claimed by several scientists and medical practitioners, though Morton was officially recognized by Congress as the rightful inventor. Still, Morton remained haunted by others' claims, and shortly before his death grew so incensed he threw himself into a pond in New York City.

The creators of the monument sidestepped these competing claims by topping the 35 foot pillar not with a likeness of Morton, Warren, or any other 19th century scientist, but with the Bible's Good Samaritan, here represented as a dour man sporting a long robe, lush beard, and turban. On his knee sprawls a sparsely clothed youth, seemingly unconscious. The religious tale speaks to the relief of suffering.

While the City was enthusiastic about the monument, local luminaries were less enamored. Mark Twain wrote, "There in Boston is a monument to the man who discovered anesthesia; many people are aware…that that man didn't discover it at all, but stole the discovery from another man. Is this truth mighty, and will it prevail? Ah, no, my hearers, the monument is made of hardy material, but the lie it tells will outlast it a million years."

Dr. Oliver Wendall Holmes was more concise. Referencing the competing claims of ether-enthusiastic doctors, he noted it was a monument "to ether–or either."

---

Four reliefs around the base of the monument play fast and loose with the scientific, the religious, and the historical. Look closely and you'll spot scenes depicting a patient tended by doctors in a mix of classical Roman robes, a Civil War soldier having his leg amputated, an Angel of Mercy descending from heaven, and a woman representing Science seated next to Mary and baby Jesus.

# HAYDEN HOUSE PLAQUE

*Explosive commitment to the cause*

*66 Phillips Street*
*Private home, interior cannot be visited*
*Red Line or Green Line/Park Street*

**B**eacon Hill is home to Boston's ritziest addresses, but its modern reputation belies a history of hardship and heroism. In the 1850s, this neighborhood was home to a thriving community of escaped slaves seeking freedom in the North. The national conversation around slavery was becoming only more fraught in the lead-up to the Civil War, and New England was not an entirely safe harbor.

The Fugitive Slave Law of 1850 empowered Southerners to seek the return of escaped slaves without due process. Federal marshals were given powers to force compliance; payments incentivized commissioners to ship suspects south; those who obstructed the process could be slapped with fines and prison time.

Lewis and Harriet Hayden, escaped slaves themselves, were not deterred. After fleeing Kentucky in the 1840s, they settled in Boston by 1850 and opened a boarding house and used-clothing store on Beacon Hill. The Haydens' home was one of the most active safe houses along the Underground Railroad.

In response to the Fugitive Slave Law, Boston abolitionists formed a Committee of Vigilance and Safety to provide shelter, food, clothing, and passage to escaped slaves. The Committee's minutes from 1850–1860 list hundreds of people the Haydens protected and provided for; Lewis was on the Committee.

In 1850, the Haydens welcomed escaped slaves William and Ellen Craft, whose path to freedom was especially audacious. Ellen was light-skinned enough to "pass" as white. In order to escape Georgia, Ellen disguised herself as a white man and pretended William was her slave. They kept up the ruse, hiding in plain sight, through hotels, trains, and boats heading north. Slave catchers tracked the Crafts to the Hayden house and demanded their return. This was Boston's first test of the Fugitive Slave Law.

Lewis stood his ground, declaring that below his feet were kegs of gunpowder; if the slave hunters came in to claim the Crafts, Lewis vowed to blow up the whole place. According to *The Liberator*, Boston's antislavery newspaper, the U.S. Marshal abandoned his pursuit of the Crafts because "He knew that the road to hell lay over Lewis Hayden's threshold; and the cost to him would be rather more than the Slave Power would be ready to make up to him; and so the Crafts remained quietly, and when they got ready, they went to England."

# ETHER DOME

*Home of pain relief*

55 Fruit Street, 4th Floor
Enter via the Massachusetts General Hospital lobby and follow signs for the
Bulfinch Building
8am–9pm daily except when booked for conferences
Call 617 724 8009 to check availability
Red Line/Charles-MGH

The Ether Dome at the top of Massachusetts General Hospital is the operating theater where anesthesia was introduced to the public for the first time. On 16 October 1846, a dentist named William T.G. Morton administered ether to Gilbert Abbott, who was suffering from a vascular neck tumor. Surgeon John Collins Warren then cut out the tumor under Abbott's jaw, with the patient reporting no pain, only scratching sensations. Warren turned to the room of spectators and declared, "Gentlemen, this is no humbug."

In the early days of modern medicine, operating theaters were often built at the top of hospitals to maximize natural light – and to minimize the amount of screaming that reached other medical wards.

The room features stadium seating, along with a grab bag of historical miscellany. Behind glass is a human skeleton, a common teaching tool in the 19th century. While the origins of this skeleton are unknown, it is visible in daguerreotypes as far back as 1847.

A plaster cast of Apollo – god of healing – looms over the operating area. Technically known as "Apollo Belvedere," this is a copy of a Roman marble sculpture, itself likely a copy of a Greek original. Today, the Roman statue stands in the Vatican Museums. The Dome's Apollo took up residence in the 1840s, a gift from Edward Everett, holder of many illustrious positions including Harvard President, U.S. Secretary of State, and Senator.

Oddly, the room also contains an Egyptian sarcophagus and mummy. In life, he was Padihershef, a stonemason and resident of 7th century Thebes. In 1823, the City of Boston gifted Padihershef to the hospital, which considered it "an appropriate ornament of the operating room," a function it still serves.

On the front wall of the theater hangs "Ether Day, 1846," a painting of the surgery along with a bevy of mustachioed medical men looking on in various states of rapture. Completed in 2001, artists Warren and Lucia Prosperi based their composition on a full-scale re-creation involving 20 people associated with MGH decked out in costumes and make-up supplied by Emerson College's Department of Performing Arts.

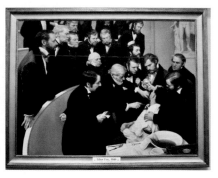

# THE SACRED COD

*For Cod and country*

*24 Beacon Street*

The General Laws of Massachusetts Part 1, Title 1, Chapter 2, Section 13 declares, "The cod shall be the fish or fish emblem and the historic and continuing symbol of the commonwealth."

And so it has.

That is why, hanging above the viewing gallery of the House Chamber in the Massachusetts State House, is a 4 foot, 11 inch, 80 pound wooden codfish.

The cod fishing industry is credited with building the economy of Massachusetts – not for nothing has the state's most popular vacation destination been called Cape Cod since 1602 – and thus the fish elicits religious devotion.

While the current State House codfish sculpture dates to 1784, it is the third iteration. The first is spottily tracked in the history books but, mythical or not, is believed to have burnt inside the State House in 1747. (An 1895 Committee on History of the Emblem of the Codfish refers to the first codfish as "a dim tradition that in the primitive House of Assembly of the Province there hung a codfish"). The next codfish was destroyed around 1773, presumably by the British seeking to strike a blow to the morale of the Boston revolutionaries.

Today's cod was donated by wealthy Boston businessman John Rowe and has proven durable. In 1798, when the government moved from the Old State House to the current State House atop Beacon Hill, the cod was wrapped in the American flag and solemnly paraded through the streets of Boston (a procession re-enacted by costumed tour guides in 2023 on the 225th anniversary).

In 1895, the House was moved to a new chamber and, after much deliberation, the body decided no cod could be left behind. With a theatrical flourish, the legislators again wrapped the cod in the flag and – this time protected by the Sergeant-at-Arms – delivered it to its new home.

There have been close calls. In 1933, pranksters from the Harvard Lampoon secreted the codfish out of the State House in a flower box, prompting a frantic 50-hour search. Its height was raised thereafter. In 1941, a metal collection drive requested the donation of the cod, not realizing it was made of pine, not aluminum. In 1968, UMASS students removed the fish in protest of a piece of legislation.

Despite it all, the codfish remains powerfully evocative. In the words of the 1895 committee:

"Humble the subject and homely the design; yet this painted image bears on its finny front a majesty greater than the dignity that art can lend to graven gold or chiselled marble…It typifies to the citizens of the Commonwealth and of the world the founding of a State. It commemorates Democracy. It celebrates the rise of free institutions. It emphasizes progress. It epitomizes Massachusetts."

---

If time permits, check out the chandelier in the State House Senate chambers, which features a "Holy" Mackerel sculpture above its central chandelier.

# CONGREGATIONAL LIBRARY AND ARCHIVES

*Preserving the Puritan past*

*14 Beacon Street*
*Email ref@14beacon.org or call 617 523 0491 to make an appointment to visit the reading room and stacks*
*Red Line or Green Line/Park Street*

The Congregational Library is an archive bursting with records and historic miscellany documenting the Congregational Church tradition, a denomination with deep roots in American history.

The Congregationalists are the intellectual descendants of the Puritans – more commonly known to Americans as the Pilgrims. The Puritan tradition arose to counter the power of the Church of England; its adherents believed in decentralized worship, with local churches functioning free from hierarchy, tradition, and political corruption.

In 1620, the Pilgrims who boarded the *Mayflower* were seeking a place they could realize the democratic ideal of a self-ruling congregation governed by the choices of its members, with Jesus – not royalty or the Pope – at its head. The centuries have seen the rise and fall of many sects, and the Library houses 225,000 documents and artifacts that track this complicated history.

The archives hold a piece of Plymouth Rock – the landing spot of the Pilgrims – and wood from their church in England. An original copy of the "Cambridge Platform," dating from 1649, lays out colonial ministers' vision of autonomous churches. The archive contains 15,000 sermons, from the late 17th century to modern times, as well as an enormous collection of New England church records, including the 1706 baptismal record for Benjamin Franklin.

One exquisite piece is the Eliot Bible, the first Bible printed in America. Dating from the early 1660s, the Bible is written in the Native American Algonquin language. The author, Reverend John Eliot, was known as the "Apostle to the Indians" and spent 10 years translating the Old and New Testaments. Eliot organized converted Native Americans into so-called "Praying Towns" throughout Massachusetts.

He is featured on the Library's exterior bas-reliefs, which represent the core principles of Congregationalism. Eliot is shown preaching to Native Americans in their own language in the 1640s. Other reliefs show the signing of the Mayflower Compact, the Pilgrims holding a Sunday service, and the founding of Harvard.

Also, be sure to ask to see the Archive's marvelously bizarre 1976 Marvel comic book in which famous Puritan clergyman Cotton Mather appears as a time-traveling witch-hunter who faces off against Spiderman and the Scarlet Witch.

---

Eliot's first sermon in Algonquin is believed to have occurred in present-day Newton, at the wigwam of a Chief Waban, who converted to Christianity. The supposed site of the wigwam is marked by a memorial to Eliot and can be visited at 99 Magnolia Avenue.

# LAW STATUES AT JOHN ADAMS COURTHOUSE

*Legal standing*

*1 Pemberton Square*
*Green Line or Blue Line/Government Center*

The John Adams Courthouse is a gorgeous building, hidden on all sides from passersby due to poor city planning. The courthouse was built in 1893, part of the neighborhood's turnover from residential to commercial and government buildings.

The Courthouse was conceived as basically a public thoroughfare: the ornate interior was designed for Bostonians to walk through as they climbed to the State House above or descended to shops below.

These dreams were dashed when an enormous, curved office building (soullessly called Center Plaza) was built directly around the Courthouse in the 1960s, sequestering it from sunlight and city dwellers.

The lobby thus has the hush and dim lighting of a medieval church, an impression reinforced by the 16 life-size statues that line the walls. Each allegorical figure represents an idea related to Law and Justice. They are perched like saints and prophets, looming slightly forward, seemingly to intimidate the lawyers, judges, and jurors that pass beneath.

A small sign identifies each figure. The only one who might look familiar is Legislation – a heavily bearded Moses. But where are his tablets? The sculptor, Domingo Mora, chose to forego the traditional representation of the Ten Commandments and instead placed the Roman numbers I through X directly onto his cloak. Moses instead holds a piece of parchment – presumably the legislation that derives from these godly strictures.

In contrast to Moses's heavy frown, Innocence is uplifting and beautiful: a young woman with flowing hair, topped by a flowered crown. A lamb peeks out at her right, and she is washing her hands clean in a basin, suggesting the legal process can restore innocence even to those stained by crime.

No such luck for Guilt, who is heavily robed and scowling. Look closely – but don't get too close: he is hiding a dagger behind his raised hands. Good thing his neighbor, Punishment, stands at the ready with shackles and a sizable ax.

Other details to note as you take in the coterie: Religion is sporting a nun's cap (called a coif) and holding a Bible fit for thumping. Right is holding a scroll with 12 Roman numerals, a reference to the Laws of the 12 Tables, the backbone of Rome's legal system. And Justice isn't holding scales as she usually would, though they are there, dangling as a rather fetching necklace.

# THE GARDEN OF PEACE

*A memorial for the murdered*

*Behind 100 Cambridge Street, off Somerset Street*
*Red Line or Green Line/Park Street*

The Garden of Peace opened in 2004 to honor victims of homicide and to inspire peace in those whose loved ones were lost to violence. It's quite an ambition for a park of only 7,000 square feet.

The garden is as much sculpture as landscape. Designed by Catherine Melina, every element symbolizes a stage of grief or recovery, with a concluding message of hope. The garden's path begins next to a large hunk of black granite called "Tragic Density," which makes physical the crushing weight of grief.

A streambed lined with river stones is kept dry. According to the official government description of the garden, "A stream should be full of water, the life-giver; but this stream is dry with only the victims' names to remind us of the lives that were taken."

Hundreds of the stones are etched with the names, birthdays, and dates of death of the murdered. Most will be unfamiliar, though two stand out: Robert and John F. Kennedy were both honored at the request of their brother Edward Kennedy, who at the time of the garden's opening was a U.S. senator and who donated towards its construction. The names of victims who were honored after 2010 appear not on river stones but on the walls of seating areas within the garden – a creative solution for a tight space. For those honored after 2020, names are placed on small steel plaques demarcating the edge of the garden.

The experience of the garden is meant to culminate in a pool and waterfall, the water symbolizing vitality and the possibility of healing. However, since its inception, the park has struggled to keep water flowing due to budget constraints and upkeep. Still, it is easy enough to imagine.

From this pool emerges the most eye-catching aspect of the garden, a lovely sculpture by Judy Kensley McKie called "Ibis Ascending" which shows three of the lissome birds rising skyward peacefully, indicating the transcendence of violence and sorrow. In 1990, McKie's son was stabbed to death in Cambridge.

The creation of the garden was the result of the efforts of an organization known as Parents of Murdered Children, which struggled to raise the necessary attention and dollars to get the project off the ground. Each September, new names are added to the garden in an annual "Honor Program," a depressing reminder of the persistence of violence.

# COMPETING CLAIMS TO THE FIRST TELEPHONE CALL

## *Crossed wires*

*5 Exeter Place and 15 Sudbury Street, just outside the JFK Federal Building*
*Green Line or Blue Line/Government Center*

On 10 March 1876, in Boston, Alexander Graham Bell made the world's first phone call, beckoning his assistant Thomas Watson with the words "Mr. Watson, come here. I want to see you."

It is a defining moment in history, yet the city makes hardly any recognition of the moment: there are no statues, yearly re-enactments, or telephone t-shirts.

Or perhaps the city makes *too much* recognition of the moment, for within half a mile of each other, two different sites bear plaques claiming to mark the site of the first telephone call.

What is going on?

To start, Bell grew up fascinated by the human voice. As an adult, Bell saw himself as a reformer of education for the deaf, believing the hearing-impaired could learn to speak and live without accommodation. He was against sign language and advocated for a system of "Visual Speech" his father had created. Bell moved to Boston to work at a premier school for the deaf and, as a devout tinkerer, benefited from the city's vibrant community of telegraph engineers.

Bell and Watson ran experiments in sound in a rented space above a telegraph factory at 109 Court Street – an address that no longer exists but was near today's JFK Federal Building. Bell first transferred sound over wire at that address. It was the "boing" of a spring.

And thus, a small granite marker stands by the roadside with a likeness of their contraption claiming it as the birthplace of the telephone.

However, each night Bell and Watson packed their rudimentary telephone and worked at a boarding house on Exeter Street, a 10-minute walk away. It is there the famous words were spoken over a wire – actual human language transmitted for the first time.

Thus, in 1916, the Bostonian Society and New England Telephone and Telegraph Company installed a plaque commemorating "the first complete and intelligible sentence by telephone" – a rather specific claim.

Bell himself was present at the unveiling of the second marker, giving it a bit more weight in claiming the distinction.

## Another phone-related plaque

Still hankering for phone-related plaques? Head to 700 Main Street in Cambridge, where a marker commemorates the first long-distance two-way telephone call. "Long distance" turns out to be rather relative: Watson was there in Cambridge and Bell was over in Boston.

# STEAMING TEA KETTLE

*Tea for ten thousand*

*63–65 Court Street*
*Green Line or Blue Line/Government Center*

**O**ff a narrow building near Boston City Hall hangs a bizarre historical artifact: an enormous golden tea kettle, steaming away while pedestrians tread the sidewalk below.

This brass-and-gold leaf kettle was forged for the Oriental Tea Company in 1873 by Hicks and Badger, Boston's premier coppersmith. The kettle was an advertisement for the tea room below and appealed particularly to the city's newly arrived immigrants – no English was needed to understand what was sold within.

An inscription on the side of the kettle commemorates a marketing stunt from 1875. The company asked the public to guess the volume of the sign, then held a public demonstration on New Year's Day to fill and measure its capacity. Ten thousand people filled Scollay Square (now City Hall) as the city's Sealer of Weights and Measures oversaw the process. A judge was on hand to lend even further legitimacy to the affair.

Before the liquid flowed, for an additional touch of flair, eight children and one tall man climbed out of the kettle, much to the surprise of the crowd.

When the deed was done, a blackboard tally reflected the final result, which was later stamped on the side of the kettle: 227 gallons, 2 quarts, 1 pint, and 3 gills. (A gill is a historical measure defined as one-fourth of a pint.)

Eight winners were named and received a chest containing five pounds of tea each.

The sign remained a calling card for the Oriental Tea Company. An 1890 advertisement in the Boston Evening Standard reads: "Oriental Tea Co. Importers of Oriental Male Berry Java (best coffee known) Teas and coffees to suit every purse and every taste, retailed at wholesale prices. Goods always uniform, always pure. Extra choice grades a specialty. Sign of Big Tea Kettle. 87 Court Street."

The kettle was moved several times due to the development of today's Government Center. In 2016, a vehicle – likely a passing truck – damaged the teapot, which required removal for repairs. Happily, it has reclaimed its place and continues to steam away.

---

A specialized mechanism on the inside of the pot creates puffs of steam that emanate from the kettle's spout, especially visible on winter days.

# DONKEY STATUE

*"I fell in love with a donkey"*

*45 School Street*
*Red Line or Green Line/Park Street*

**B**oston preservationist Roger Webb is recognized as the founder of several nonprofits devoted to documenting and protecting buildings of historical significance. Until his death in 2019, he was a leader in saving and reinventing Boston landmarks, including Faneuil Hall and the Old City Hall, which was abandoned in the 1970s for Boston's current brutalist government center one block away.

A lesser-known achievement of Roger's: in 1998, he successfully managed to foist on this historic city – despite its protestations – a life-size bronze statue of an Italian donkey.

In the mid-1990s, Roger was in Florence exploring a statuary shop when a special creature caught his eye. In Roger's words, from a 2015 letter he wrote to the Boston Preservation Alliance, "Traveling in Italy I fell in love with a donkey…My eye fell upon a life-size donkey hidden behind a large statue of a hog and Michelangelo's David with a saintly woman kneeling in prayer. The donkey looked at me and we fell in love. I pictured this little donkey in Boston on The Freedom Trail – perhaps in front of Old City Hall."

Roger surmised that the donkey would be beloved by children, especially those exploring nearby historic sites. He bought the statue for under $10,000, arranged for it to be shipped, and began lobbying for a permanent home.

City Hall was unmoved, questioning the donkey's relevance to Boston. Roger was a determined man and suggested to the authorities that the donkey might belong in front of the Old City Hall, which is built on the site of America's first public school. He argued that a young Ben Franklin (a statue of whom was already erected) and other children likely rode their donkeys to school and parked them in the courtyard. He received a resounding no.

Roger regrouped, stored the large statue in his daughter's garage, and tried another tack: from 1865 to 1970, the Old City Hall was dominated by Democratic mayors, he reasoned. What better symbol than the Democratic Donkey to stand in its courtyard?

Amazingly, Roger won approval.

He was soon receiving questions about what acknowledgement Republicans might earn and, rather than commissioning a GOP elephant counterpart, he convinced a cousin to sculpt two footprints in front of the donkey, with the words "STAND IN OPPOSITION" and two cartoon elephants.

# "CITY CARPET"

## *Hopscotch through history*

*Sidewalk in front of 45 School Street*
*Red Line or Green Line/Park Street*

Boston, renowned for its world-class universities, has a lesser-known distinction in the history of education: it was home to America's first public school: Boston Latin School was established on 23 April 1635 – one year before Harvard College.

Boston Latin's original wooden building occupied a plot on School Street. It was removed in 1745 to expand King's Chapel, which remains in place. On the sidewalk just down from the church, however, the history of Boston Latin is celebrated in a literally playful manner: an intricate hopscotch board is set into the pavement and features children at play.

The vibrant scenes show students in decidedly unacademic settings – kite-flying, rolling hoops, jumping rope, playing marbles, drawing, swinging, and generally running amok – but the inscriptions offer a buttoned-up celebration of the school's most distinguished alumni: Samuel Adams, John Hancock, Charles Bulfinch, and Ralph Waldo Emerson. Five signers of the Declaration of Independence attended Boston Latin – Adams, Hancock, Robert Treat Paine, William Hooper, and Benjamin Franklin (who notably dropped out).

The school's Latin motto, which translates to "Work conquers all – opportunity for all" also stands in contrast to the playful theme.

At its founding, Boston Latin School's student body was exclusively male but was open to boys of all levels of wealth and status, a shockingly democratic experiment at the time. Female students didn't join Boston Latin's ranks until 1972.

Reverend John Cotton was instrumental in the founding of the school and modeled its curriculum on the Free Grammar School of Boston, England, which centered on the study of the humanities and emphasized Latin and Greek. Even today, the school's mascot is the wolf, a modern adaptation of the she-wolf who suckled Romulus and Remus. The she-wolf herself is pictured in the mural between the words "Latin" and "School."

The mosaic was created in 1983 by artist Lilli Ann Killen Rosenberg. Working in ceramic, stone, brick, and concrete, she cheekily included a decidedly local reference among the alphabet that provides a frame to the hopscotch board: the tile after "G" shows a very specific insect – the Golden Grasshopper weathervane atop nearby Faneuil Hall.

# CHARLES DICKENS DOOR

*That magical voice*

*Omni Parker House*
*60 School Street*
*Red Line or Green Line/Park Street*

The Omni Parker House is a Boston landmark. Since its founding in 1855, it has gone through countless rounds of renovation and housed many famous guests. Few were famous enough, though, to warrant the removal and loving preservation of their hotel room door.

Yet, in a basement hallway just outside the hotel gym, the door to #138 and #139 hangs behind protective plastic in honor of the man that once called these rooms home: Charles Dickens.

The door was saved from demolition by a workman, put in storage for 90 years, then returned to the hotel in 2015.

At Christmas time, it is adorned by a wreath in honor of *A Christmas Carol*.

At the peak of his fame, Charles Dickens came to the U.S. for a reading tour in 1867–1868. His base of operations was a suite in downtown Boston selected by Harvey Parker, the founder of the Omni Parker House.

Dickens had visited the U.S. once before, in 1842, and left with a bad impression. He was disgusted by slavery and found the American manner vulgar. Two and a half decades later, he was tempted back by the promise of packed rooms and unabashed adoration, and chose Boston as his jumping off point out of loyalty to his local literary friends, including Longfellow and Emerson. He arrived on 19 November, checked in – and was immediately unhappy.

According to his tour manager, George Dolby, the hotel waiters left the sitting room door to Dickens's rooms ajar so that guests could gawk at the literary celebrity. "This curiosity made an unpleasant impression in his mind, and caused him to regret that he had not adhered to his original determination never to visit America again; for, he said, 'These people have not in the least changed during the last five and twenty years – they are doing now exactly what they were doing then.' But here I reminded him that he had not been three hours in the country...."

Once he was out on stage, Dickens's feelings softened. The crowds came. The theatricality of Dickens's style was noted by reviewers. The *New York Daily Tribune* praised, "that magical voice which will be recognized wherever it is heard in America as the voice of a great author, and of the greatest, perhaps (certainly in versatility of power the greatest), that has ever charmed our Western World."

## A mirror from Dickens's room

A mirror from Dickens's suite of rooms was also saved and can be visited on the hotel's mezzanine level.

## The marble tabletop of Ho Chi Minh

Dickens is not the only famous name who spent time at the Omni Parker: before he was a revolutionary leader, Ho Chi Minh worked as a baker in the hotel's kitchen from 1911–1913. The marble tabletop he used is still in place today and was visited by the Prime Minister of Vietnam in 2022.

# PROVINCE HOUSE STEPS

*Nine steps to British rule*

Next to 45 Province Street
Red Line or Green Line/Park Street

Nine steps are all that remain of a once famous house of great power: The Province House, the residence of Massachusetts Colony's Royal Governors from 1715 to the American Revolution.

In 1679, local merchant Peter Sergeant constructed perhaps the grandest house in Boston. It was imposing and oozed wealth: a three-story construction of bricks imported from Holland, a 51 foot long front facade, double chimneys, a grand staircase, and a 75 square foot lawn with tiered gardens and orchards behind. (No, these steps aren't the grand staircase – these led to the back stables.) The house, too, was perfectly geographically situated between the bustling industry of the harbor and the centers of political power.

Upon Sergeant's death in 1716, the government purchased the home for 2,300 pounds and made several alterations, including new iron fences and tapestries fit for royal receptions. A Royal Coat of Arms was installed over the front door (it can still be visited today at the nearby Old State House). In 1727, the House of Representatives earmarked funds for further renovations: "That the Great lower Room in the Front be wainscotted; after the best and newest Fashion, that the Ceiling in that Room be lowered, and the doors altered, That the windows be altered and sash Lights made throughout the House, the Windows to be Cased several of them with Seats…"

Six governors called Province House home. While the Province House survived the Revolutionary War unscathed, the new State of Massachusetts was anxious to divest itself of the property and passed ownership to the Massachusetts General Hospital, intending it to be used as a medical facility. Finding it unfit, Mass General rented the space out, and it was reinvented several times – as a tavern, opera house, minstrel hall, temporary lodging, and trade shops. In 1916, the property was sold to Olympia Theatres, Inc., which promptly planned demolition.

While there was opposition – led primarily by antiquarian William Sumner Appleton, who stated that, "Some people…consider it would have been superior even to Mt. Vernon. No house of this period built of brick in the grand style exists anywhere in an American city." – the house was gone by 1922, except for these stairs and the remains of the fireplaces, bricks of which were incorporated into the new building.

# STOCK EXCHANGE STAIRCASE

㉒

*A climb to remember*

*53 State Street*
*Lobby open during regular business hours*
*Green Line/Government Center*

Heading toward 53 State Street from any distance today, you'll see a relatively soulless glassed-in office tower. Yet, as you approach at street level, you'll see an oddly-shaped portion of the building that seems decidedly pre-modern. That's precisely because it is: this pink granite wall dates back to the 11 story building that was constructed on this site in 1891.

While that scale may seem modest now, by the standards of the late 19th century it was a behemoth, decked out with steam heating, electricity, and – according to a survey of Boston buildings – "three large and powerful passenger elevators."

The building, designed by the premier architecture firm of Peabody and Stearns, was home to the Boston Stock Exchange – a large financial institution that brought together so many professionals under a single roof that it is believed to have been the most populated building in all of New England.

"The crowning feature of this immense building is the rooms of the stock exchange...The great chamber of the exchange is 115 feet long 50 feet wide...the interior decorations are in white and yellow, with dignified Corinthian pillars...Leading from this larger room is the bond room with its massive black Tennessee marble fireplace."

Sadly, these elegant temples to commerce were all destroyed in the 1980s when developers, intent on expansion and modernization, bought the building. However, one architectural marvel remains in place: the original 1891 stairway from the building's grand lobby. After the 510 foot tall skyscraper was completed in 1985, the broad marble stairs were reinstalled into the glassed-in atrium just as they were.

For many years, the staircase led to nowhere – more a historic art piece than a practical piece of architecture. However, when the *Boston Globe* relocated its offices into the current complex, the staircase reclaimed its function. Still, it is commonly blocked off with ropes – a solid memorial to a bygone era.

The juxtaposition of the ornate staircase and the spare metal and glass of the office tower is jarring to behold.

# THE ANCIENT AND HONORABLE ARTILLERY COMPANY OF MASSACHUSETTS MUSEUM

## *Military miscellany*

*4th floor inside Faneuil Hall*
*9am to 3pm daily*
*Green Line/Government Center*

F aneuil Hall is Boston's most famous tourist trap, but hidden three floors up is a quiet gallery that preserves the history of the mightily named Ancient and Honorable Artillery Company of Massachusetts. The Company began as a militia in 1638 and is the oldest chartered military organization in the United States. With the creation of the National Guard and the professionalization of the U.S. military, the Company became a fraternal organization dedicated to "preserving the historic and patriotic traditions of our city, Commonwealth and Nation."

Company members have served in every Massachusetts colonial war and U.S. conflict since its founding. Four U.S. Presidents were members, including John F. Kennedy.

The group's Headquarters and Armory have been in Faneuil Hall since 1746; the creaky floors and sheer volume of items on display speak to this history. The walls of the Armory are crammed with a random assortment of swords, firearms, drums, flags, canes, portraits, and munitions. Uniforms of various origins and dustiness are arranged higgledy-piggledy.

A seven foot tall carving of the Massachusetts State Seal hangs at the front of the room. It dates to 1897 and is made from a single piece of wood. At the back of the room, a beautifully preserved staircase ascends to the Commander's Quarters. It was built in 1937. The 13 steps honor the colonies that ratified the Constitution, in order of ratification – Delaware first to Rhode Island last.

The Museum Room is a military cabinet of curiosities. According to its elegantly calligraphed label, a frame holds 52 Native American arrowheads collected on Cape Cod from 1859–60.

A display case holds a collection of souvenir bricks gouged out of vaguely historic buildings: "This brick was taken from the old tomb of Gen. U.S. Grant" (also known as President Ulysses S. Grant); "Brick taken from the wall of Libby Prison Richmond VA…where more than 30,000 Union Prisoners of War…were imprisoned during the War of the Rebellion 1861-5" (also known as the Civil War.) Other bricks come from chapels, the Old Province House (see p. 55), a tavern George Washington visited, and the engine room at Harpers Ferry, where abolitionist John Brown famously tried to spark a slave revolt in 1859.

# GREENWAY CAROUSEL

*Ride a skunk*

*191 Atlantic Avenue*
*Blue Line/Aquarium*

The Greenway Carousel was unveiled in 2013 as part of the Rose Kennedy Greenway, a park built atop underground highways.

The carousel is both a child's amusement and a serious work of art. Handcrafted by sculptor Jeff Briggs of Newburyport, MA and vibrantly painted by artist Bill Rogers, the custom carousel forgoes the expected flouncy horses in favor of 14 fauna indigenous to the Boston area, including a few that are less conventionally beautiful than your standard ride.

To determine which animals to include, third- and fourth-graders contributed drawings of what animals they'd like to see. Some were no-brainers: the lobster, the Harbor seal, the cod. The right whale is encrusted with barnacles and – look close – the pole is a spray of water from its blowhole. Others were more subtle: the grasshopper is a historical nod to the weathervane atop nearby Faneuil Hall. Some seemed like good concepts but posed challenges for actual rideability, like the Peregrine falcon and three local species of butterfly.

According to Briggs, carousel design is challenging because of the need to balance engineering considerations, regulatory requirements, and pure artistry. "The tricky part is the actual safety inspection, which only happens once the carousel is up!" he noted.

Winged creatures are especially hard. Briggs positioned the butterfly wings fully upright, wrapped around the pole ("I crossed my fingers the inspector would okay that one"), while the falcon is tipped sideways with wings stretched high and low.

Briggs studied real animals closely to ensure verisimilitude. When he needed to design a seal that could provide back support, he spent time with Harbor seals to see if their tails could flex upward in a way that matched his plan.

A sea turtle, too, posed an unexpected problem: laid flat, it would take up two pole positions in the carousel's limited space. Briggs headed to the New England Aquarium to consult Myrtle the Turtle. "I was on a little raft, and she looked at me and went down – but when she turned to go she was so thick! I never knew! I turned to the guy and said, 'She's pretty big through, huh?" and the guy said, 'Yeah…she's fat.'" Once he realized there was plenty of room for a rider, Briggs had his solution: he sculpted the turtle sideways in mid-swim.

A few children suggested a sea monster, which went against the assignment of real animals. Briggs dove into historical research about a legendary "Sea Monster of Gloucester" and discovered that experts suspected a real, disconcertingly long oarfish. It made the cut.

When asked why he chose to include a skunk, Briggs laughed heartily. "It's got the ick factor!"

# THE BOSTON STONE

*A simple mill stone or the center of it all?*

*9 Marshall Street*
*Green Line/Haymarket*

**H**idden down an unassuming alley and embedded into a typically Boston red brick wall, a 2 foot wide, round granite stone with a hole drilled in the center sits at street level, just beside a rather uninspiring fire hose intake connection. The stone sits atop a base inscribed "Boston Stone 1737."

There is much debate about the significance – or lack of significance – of the Boston Stone, though it is generally agreed that nothing notable related to it happened in 1737.

It is thought to have been imported from England in 1700 by Thomas Childs, the owner of a paint mill that stood near the current site. Childs would have used the stone to grind material into paint pigments. Though Childs died in 1706, the paint mill stood until 1836 and, during its demolition, the stone was purportedly unearthed and incorporated into the base of the new construction.

An oft-repeated theory is that the Boston Stone was used by surveyors and city planners as the geographic center of Boston and that road markers reflect distance from the painterly rock, similar to the famed London Stone. However, historic milestones used Boston's Old State House – several blocks away from the Boston Stone – as their reference point.

Others suspect that the Boston Stone is a ruse cooked up by a Scottish businessman looking to draw customers to his out-of-the-way ale and cheese shop in the early 1800s. The proprietor wanted a geographic reference point to lure attention and claimed inspiration from the London Stone.

Indeed, whether a brilliant stroke of early advertising or not, visitors today can experience some of the same: just around the corner from the mystery stone, The Boston Stone Gift Shop offers Red Sox tchotchkes and Boston-themed Christmas ornaments galore.

Further, a bar at 147 Hanover Street called The Point cheekily contends that the true Boston Stone resides in its bathroom. The restroom door reads, "The Cornerstone of Boston: Inside the first stone laid in Boston."

# TRADE CLASSES AT NORTH BENNET STREET SCHOOL

BENNET STREET SCHOOL

(26)

*Handy and crafty*

*150 North Street*
*Visit nbss.edu/community-education for upcoming classes*
*Green Line or Orange Line/North Station*

© North Bennet Street School

North Bennet Street School is America's first and oldest trade school. Founded in 1881, the school was a charitable endeavor aimed at training immigrants in skilled manual labor that would allow them to acclimate to America and to find meaningful work. Even in today's digital age, the school's education is pleasingly focused on the physical and practical.

The school's founder, Pauline Agassiz Shaw, adopted a Swedish method known as "Educational Sloyd," which is characterized by teaching vocational skills through projects that grow increasingly difficult and complex, and build upon one another. (*Slöjd* is "craft" in Swedish.)

But the educational approach stands out for the fact that it wasn't solely intended to develop skills valuable to trade; Sloyd instruction is founded on the belief that teaching through doing – especially doing woodwork – leads to personal, mental, and moral development as well as a rich curiosity about the world.

A North Bennet teacher named Lizzie Woodward put it succinctly in 1893: "[B]ooks alone cannot restore that balance of mind and body from which purity of thought and life is derived." The school's motto today puts it even more succinctly, "A good life, built by hand."

Today, the school is home to nine full-time training programs in intriguingly specific crafts – from bookbinding to cabinetry, piano restoration to violin making ("you'll build six violins and a viola.") There is also a plethora of one-off options for the dabbler. North Bennet offers over 120 "community education" classes that delve deep into skills you may never have known you needed: paper conservation, spoon carving, broom making, and "harpsichord voicing" – the art/science of adjusting how a harpsichord string is plucked in response to pressure on the keys.

Courses are taught in the school's handsome North End facility, formerly the City of Boston's printing plant and a police station.

## A shop for handiwork by the students themselves

For those who don't want to delve as deep into craft esoterica, a shop inside the school offers handiwork by the students themselves. Pick up an impeccably detailed maple-cherry-black walnut inlaid cutting board, handmade notebooks, or a nifty hand-threaded screw nutcracker. You won't be able to buy a violin, though: those the students sell themselves.

# MINI VENICE'S PALAZZO DUCALE

## 27

*A model teacher*

*Inside the North End Branch Library*
*25 Parmenter Street*
*Monday, Tuesday, and Thursday 10am–6pm; Wednesday 12pm–8pm; Friday and*
*Saturday 9am–5pm*
*Orange Line/Haymarket*

The North End celebrates its history as Boston's Italian neighborhood, and beyond all the touristy cannoli shops and pasta places, there is an artwork that transports viewers to 16th century Venice.

The local library is home to an enormous, highly detailed scale model of Venice's historic seat of government, the Palazzo Ducale, or Doge's Palace. The diorama is the work of Henrietta Gardner Macy, who in 1878 founded a kindergarten class in Boston's North End. After several years of teaching the children of Italian immigrants, Gardner Macy began a life of travel as a reporter for several newspapers, including the *Brooklyn Daily Eagle*.

Gardner Macy moved to Venice permanently in 1890. She kept a studio for plaster model-making in a yellow house known as Ca'Frollo and opened yet another school for impoverished children, this time in a former Augustinian convent. She became known as "The Nun of Ca'Frollo."

The library's model of the Palazzo Ducale is Gardner Macy's third rendition. She created the first to entertain a friend's sons during a summer visit. The boys died of diphtheria the next winter and, in their honor, Gardner Macy devoted three years to producing a second, larger model. This version was bought by the New York Metropolitan Museum of Art – and tragically destroyed by a fire in transit.

Gardner Macy spent several more years building the final model, which was incomplete upon her death in 1927. A friend hired artisans to complete the model then donated it to the library.

The diorama buzzes with life, as clergy, artists, politicians, gondoliers, and gentry go about their business. Created by Louise Stimson of Concord, MA, the figures brim with detail.

Keep an eye out for "The Companions of the Hose," a group of foppishly dressed young men preparing to play music. It was a real group: the *Compagnie della Calza* hosted elaborate pageants and entertainments. There is also a widow clad in black – save for her gray veil, which indicated her interest in finding another companion.

---

The library's design is modeled after a Roman villa: bookshelves and tables encircle a central courtyard and garden. The courtyard features a weathered brick walkway and a 1913 white marble bas-relief celebrating the life of Dante Alighieri.

# ALL SAINTS WAY

## 28

*A saintly pastime*

*Alley off Battery Street near intersection with Hanover Street*
*Open 1–2pm most weekdays and 9:30am–noon most weekends*
*Green Line/Haymarket*

The narrow alley between 4 and 8 Battery Street is located in a quiet stretch of the North End that tourists don't often get to, the spaghetti and cannoli shops thinning several blocks away. The alley, squeezed between two tall brick buildings, houses an unexpected attraction – part collage, part tourist trap, part museum, part shrine.

It is called "All Saints Way" and for good reason: nearly every surface is covered with images, mementos, and statues of Catholic saints.

The mastermind behind the collection is Peter Baldassari. Baldassari was raised in Boston's North End and has never left. As a child raised in the Church, he started a collection of prayer cards, which often feature gauzy pictures of saints and related prayers. His collection grew over the decades and, roughly 30 years ago, he hit upon the idea of establishing a shrine or, at least, a saint-themed cabinet of curiosities.

Lines of miniature figurines hold their hands in prayer and raise their little eyes skyward, imploring the Lord to intervene for various causes – lepers, cancers, lost items. Portraits of historic (and possibly legendary) saints and pictures of those more recently canonized share wall space alongside signs imploring visitors to love Jesus and honor these holy men and women. Crosses and angels abound, alongside dioramas and votive candles.

A homemade sign quotes an Italian saying that captures the spirit of Baldassari's attitude perfectly: "Mock all and sundry things but leave the saints alone."

Baldassari himself is often on the premises, impressing visitors with his encyclopedic knowledge of the heavenly host and recounting the provenance of various artifacts, including those sent to him from abroad. He might expound on Saint Lucy, forever depicted holding a chalice in which float her own eyes (she plucked them out so a suitor would leave her to her prayers) or Saint George, slayer of dragons. For Baldassari, each saint is a character in his own thrilling tale.

While the alley has a locked door during off-hours, many of the artifacts can still be viewed from the street, and Baldassari curates special scenes – and often beautiful flowers – above the entrance.

# CHANGE-RINGING
# AT OLD NORTH CHURCH

*Music by the numbers*

*193 Salem Street*
*Visit bellringers.scripts.mit.edu/www/ for upcoming performances*
*Visit oldnorth.com/admission-pricing/ for tours of the bell chamber*
*Green Line or Orange Line/North Station*

Old North Church was made famous as the site of Paul Revere's "one if by land, two if by sea" warning of British troops on the march. Most visitors to Boston take 10 minutes to amble through the church's boxy pews and admire a bust of George Washington, but few take the time to head upstairs to the bell-ringing chamber.

The chamber, a small brick room with ramshackle wooden doors and rickety staircases, sits two floors below the bell chamber itself. Eight thick ropes are tied to a central post, then swoop in graceful arcs and ascend through holes in the ceiling, where each is attached to a bell. The ropes each have a special black-and-red striped covering called a "sally," which protects the ringers' hands from rope burn and indicates the position of the bells above.

The eight bells – which date from 1745 and range from 620 to 1,500 pounds – are designed for a technique called "change-ringing." Regular bells hang vertically and ring when a clapper is yanked to strike the bells' sides. Change-ringing bells are mounted in a frame on a wheel; when the sally is pulled downward, the bell swings fully upside down so its mouth is facing up, then momentum rotates the bell swiftly on its wheel, causing the clapper to hit its side and resonate when the bell is again facing fully upward. This position maximizes the volume of the note.

Posted on the wall of the bell chamber is a sheet of inscrutable numbers. These are the essence of change-ringing. The technique does not produce melodies, as most church carillons do, but follows precise mathematical patterns. The unique set-up of these bells allows for greater control over the speed of ringing. Skilled change-ringers control the speed precisely to follow mathematical permutations, or changes. Thus change-ringing.

If it sounds complicated, it is. The Old North bells were the first of their kind in the U.S. and, following installation, sat unused for five years until the church reverend recruited a group of teenagers to learn the technique. Among that group was none other than a 15-year-old named Paul Revere.

Today the bells are rung by the MIT Guild of Bellringers each Sat-

Twice a year the Guild performs a full peal – an extraordinary three-hour performance, done completely from memory. A full peal is a feat of athleticism: each bell rings no less than 5,000 times.

*Angels stolen during King George's War in the 1740s*

*193 Salem Street*
*Visit oldnorth.com/admission-pricing/ for tours and hours*
*Green Line or Orange Line/North Station*

Old North is sacred ground for American history buffs, and actual sacred ground for Episcopalians. Yet this place of faith is crowned by objects of sin: four beautiful but unassuming wooden painted angels that stand atop the balcony (just in front of America's oldest pipe organ). Note that the angels contrast with the church itself: where they are colorfully painted and expressive, the church's pews and altar are all right angles and white paint.

And for good reason. The angels were never intended for Old North – or indeed for any Episcopalian church. In 1746, the foursome were on a French ship bound for a Catholic church near Quebec when they were taken by an American privateer who regarded them as the fair spoils of war. "Thy shall not steal" be damned.

In the 1740s, England and France were, as ever, fighting. The conflict was known as King George's War, though it was precipitated by a pan-European battle over who would take the throne in Austria upon the death of Emperor Charles VI. Due to a web of alliances, the British colonies were pulled into war with French Canada.

Captain Thomas Gruchy, a transplant from England and owner of Pew No. 25, was a successful mariner and merchant. In 1744, Gruchy and four other parishioners purchased a ship named Queen of Hungary to battle French and Spanish vessels at sea as privateers – essentially private citizens acting as Navy men. Gruchy was named captain, and he and his crew spent several years besting and looting the ships of competitive nations. In 1745, Gruchy took three French ships; the following year, the records of Old North (also called Christ Church) contain the following: "Whereas Mr. Robert Jenkins, Captn. Grushia, Mr. Hugh McDaniel, Mr. John Goule, Mr. John Baker, Oners of the Privater Queen of Hungary hath made a present to Christ Church in Boston, of 4 Cherubims and Two Glass Branches Taken by ye Sd. Vessele. Voted that the Branches be hung in ye body of the Church and ye Cherubims placed on ye top of the Organ"

And thus the angels ascended.

The statues themselves predate the war; it's believed they were carved in modern-day Belgium in the early 1600s. Thus, over a century of their history – who gazed upon them and where – is lost to time. Yet, for far longer they have stood watch over the parishioners – some would say plunderers – and tourists of Boston.

# BULLET MARKS ON THE GRAVE OF DANIEL MALCOM

*British bullets*

*Copp's Burying Ground, 45 Hull Street*
*Green Line or Orange Line/North Station*

Captain Daniel Malcom was an American revolutionary and a smuggler. In 1768, he protested British taxes by landing 60 casks of wine on one of the islands in Boston Harbor and bringing them ashore in secret rather than give money to the oppressor overseas.

At great risk, he publicly recounted observing the British illegally seize a boat owned by John Hancock. In his recounting, a British commander colorfully ordered his soldiers that "the first damned rascal that said a word to blow his brains out, or run him through with the bayonet."

Malcom never witnessed the American Revolution, as he died just one year after his wine caper, but his gravestone made his allegiances clear, declaring him "an Enemy to oppression and one of the foremost in opposing the Revenue Acts on America."

His insolence was not forgotten. Copp's Hill was a strategically important spot during the Revolutionary War due to its elevated position above Boston Harbor and its clear views of surrounding territory. In the Revolutionary Era, Copp's Hill stood 10 feet higher than it stands today; in the 1800s, much of its soil was carted away as landfill for nearby Mill Pond.

British soldiers built a fortification on the hill, and it was from this site the British cannons shot on Charlestown during the famous Battle of Bunker Hill. Many historians contend that, during their idle hours, soldiers used the colonists' graves for target practice.

The inscription on Malcom's grave made it an obvious favorite for the loyalists' musket balls. While the centuries have weathered the grave, the distinct pockmarks from British bullets are clear to a close observer.

---

Also in the Copp's Burying Ground is a curious tripartite headstone – the final resting place of George and Ann Worthylake and their daughter Ruth, all of whom drowned when their boat capsized in the harbor on 3 November 1718. George was the first keeper of the Boston Light, America's oldest continuously manned lighthouse. The tragedy of their death inspired an adolescent Ben Franklin, then a printer's apprentice to his brother in Boston, to compose a ballad called "The Lighthouse Tragedy," which was "wretched stuff" but "sold wonderfully," according to his *Autobiography*. The text has been lost.

# MONUMENT AND GRAVESTONE OF PRINCE HALL

## Founder of Black Freemasonry

*Copp's Burying Ground, 45 Hull Street*
*Green Line or Orange Line/North Station*

Likely born in Boston in 1735, Prince Hall was a free Black man who advocated for the abolition of slavery and equal rights at a time when most of the country was focused on breaking ties with England. Hall's political activism would have run alongside that of John Adams, John Hancock, Paul Revere, and other "Founding Fathers" whose names are taught to all American children.

While Prince Hall's name is not well known, his legacy has lived on for over 200 years in the form of Prince Hall Freemasonry – a branch of the secretive Masonic fraternal organization founded specifically for Black members.

Prince Hall was determined to become a Freemason, understanding it would be both a symbolic victory for Black rights and a platform for ongoing advocacy. Hall and 14 other men of color were initiated on 6 March 1775 by an Irish military lodge associated with the British Army on Castle William Island (today, Castle Island) in Boston Harbor.

When the Revolutionary War forced the Army out, Hall was left lodge-less. He and his compatriots applied for a formal charter from other Massachusetts Masons and were denied due to racial prejudice. This didn't stop them from meeting unofficially and calling themselves African Lodge No. 1. In time, Hall appealed to the Grand Lodge of England; in 1787, Hall's organization was officially chartered and dubbed African Lodge #459.

From there, #459 founded lodges in Rhode Island and Pennsylvania. When Hall died in 1807, the members of the African Lodges named Prince Hall Freemasonry in his honor. Over 5,000 Prince Hall lodges and 300,000 Master Masons descend from Hall's original vision.

Prince Hall Freemasons have quietly been at the center of the equal rights movement in the U.S. The group provided early support for the National Association for the Advancement of Colored People (NAACP), the country's pre-eminent civil rights organization. Jesse Jackson, Duke Ellington, Booker T. Washington, Richard Pryor, and the first Black Supreme Court Justice, Thurgood Marshall, were all Prince Hall Freemasons.

Hall's grave itself is modest, but nearby Massachusetts Masons erected a large memorial to him 88 years after his death. The broken column is a Masonic symbol reserved for particularly important "Brothers."

# GALLOPS ISLAND RADIO TRAINING CENTER MEMORIAL

## 33

*Duty done, message sent*

*529 Commercial Street*
*Green Line/Haymarket*

If you google "Gallops Island," your search results will mostly be about the Galapagos. That's because this 16 acre dot of land in the center of Boston Harbor is closed to visitors and nearly forgotten. However, tucked inside a public park on the city's shoreline, a statue of a sinking ship memorializes the island's time as a radio operator training center during World War II.

The island served many purposes over the years – first as a fishing spot for Native Americans, then as the home of a harbor pilot named John Gallop, then as an outpost for French cannons during the Revolutionary War, then as a hotel renowned for its clam chowder. It served as a quarantine hospital for newly arrived immigrants from the mid-1800s to 1937; over 33,000 people passed through in 1886 alone.

With war clouds gathering, Gallops became home to the U.S. Maritime Service Radio Training School in 1940. The 300-person staff trained civilians as radio operators destined to serve aboard vessels delivering goods to the front lines. Radio operators were essential for monitoring communications, sharing intelligence, sending out distress signals, and repairing complicated transmitters and receivers. It was intended that every ship at sea in the theaters of war should have three radio operators on board to provide 24-hour coverage.

Between 1940 and the school's closure in 1945, 5,000 men graduated from its courses. While learning Morse code was essential, building up speed and facility with code – especially in a moment of emergency – was even more so. The students were drilled through realistic simulations, which included piped-in static and background noise to obscure messages.

The U.S. Merchant Marine is often considered the unsung hero of the military; 9,521 members died in World War II, a higher proportion than any other branch. This memorial honors those who sought to keep others well supplied with food, clothing, and munitions through coordination and vigilance, all while traversing oceans in slow-moving ships – easy targets for German U-boats and Japanese submarines.

Gallops was abandoned after the war and used as a dump. In 1973 it became part of the protected Boston Harbor Islands State Park. While it is still part of the parks system, don't dare go ashore: visitors are kept away because of the presence of asbestos.

# THE GREAT MOLASSES DISASTER PLAQUE

## 34

*A wave of syrup causes devastation*

*529 Commercial Street*
*Green Line or Orange Line/North Station*

On 15 January 1919, an unseasonably warm day, a gigantic wave crashed down Boston's Commercial Street, devastating the crowded North End neighborhood. At its peak, the wave was 25 feet high and 165 feet across, traveling at a speed of 35 miles an hour. It claimed 21 lives and injured 150. Horses and dogs were swept away. Freight cars were crushed, automobiles overturned, buildings flooded and ripped from their foundations.

The wave was made of molasses – 2.3 million gallons of the sticky stuff.

At 529 Commercial Street, a 50 foot tall tank owned by the U.S. Industrial Alcohol Company had burst, likely due to temperature changes of the molasses within and the release of gases. As pressure grew, the tank strained, its rivets and steel walls shooting out violently. As the

© BPL, Public domain, via Wikimedia Commons

wave rolled forth, it collected ever more debris – including the animals themselves.

Once the initial danger had passed, a chest-high lake of molasses remained, trapping humans and animals. Police had to search for and shoot stuck horses; there was no way to free them.

The disaster could have been avoided. Locals had long noted troubling groans emanating from the tank, and local children would lap up molasses that leaked from its weak spots. Modern engineers hypothesize that the tank was meant to hold water, and thus wasn't sound to hold the denser, more viscous liquid. The company leaders knew of the tank's fragilities but chose to ignore and cover them up; they even painted the tank brown in the hopes of disguising leaks.

A civil lawsuit against the company resulted in $628,000 in damages to victims and their families. The devastation inspired many of the building construction standards that are commonplace today, including requiring engineers and architects to supply their calculations alongside their building plans.

There was another lingering legacy for decades after: the sweet smell of molasses. While time has surely exaggerated the story, North Enders insisted that under the right conditions, the aroma could still be detected even 50 years later.

While some have proposed more elaborate memorials – including a soaring arch that would mimic a side of the cylindrical holding tank – today the city's only monument to the Great Molasses Flood is a small green plaque in Langone Park, which covers much of the area originally affected.

# POTATO SHED MEMORIAL

*Really baked potatoes*

*Millers River Littoral Way*
*Green Line or Orange Line/North Station*

I t was not a good day to be a potato in Charlestown on 10 May 1962. The local railyards did a significant business in spuds: grown, harvested, and packed in Maine, the taters came off train cars here in the most Irish of American cities, both to be sold in the neighborhood (locals of a certain age remember their families loading up almost daily) and to be packed for further travels along the East Coast.

The potatoes were stored in massive sheds, which, according to the later Boston Fire Department report, gave the neighborhood its moniker "Potato Row." The storage operations and Boston and Maine Railroad yards were a major source of employment – and pride – for the local community.

But on that fateful May day, millions of pounds of potatoes were destroyed by a massive five-alarm fire – or, as the *Globe* would have it, they "were given a thorough roasting." Weather conditions made the fire particularly destructive: Warehouse 18, a two story shed, was reduced to "a half mile long, five foot high, pile of smoldering potatoes." Adjacent railcars and residential buildings were leveled.

The history is honored today on the Millers River Littoral Way, a pedestrian walkway that traces a restored wetland that flows into the Charles River. While the path tries desperately to be delightful, due to the surrounding highway overpasses, it rarely feels more than desolate. However, the Potato Shed Memorial manages to be both whimsical and poignant: four stacked potato sacks (one tumbling open) and a plaque that repeats "Potato" and "Potatoes" at various font sizes. It must be the most Bostonian memorial there is.

The heyday of the potato trade stretched from the 1800s into the 1930s. (The memorial plaque actually misstates the date of the fire, placing it in the '30s, not the '60s.) By 1962, the area was also used for storing baby food, flour, and orange juice. Fire inspectors had to warn off would-be looters that all the food was contaminated by the conflagration.

Maine's prodigious potato supply meant that the nation could still feast on tubers despite the fire, but it had two lasting effects. First, an important piece of Charlestown history was lost forever. Second, according to local residents, the smell of roasted potatoes blanketed the neighborhood for weeks.

# PRESIDENT ANDREW JACKSON'S LIPS

## *A head divided*

USS Constitution *Museum – Charlestown Navy Yard, 93 Chelsea Street
Monday–Sunday 10am–5pm
Green Line or Orange Line/North Station*

The *U.S.S. Constitution*, aka Old Ironsides, is America's most famous warship. It is the oldest commissioned Navy boat still afloat, made famous by exploits against the United Kingdom during the War of 1812. Launched in 1797, the Constitution is now a popular tourist attraction, but the ship museum – mostly an afterthought for those waiting to tour the vessel – is home to a historic artifact that speaks to America's history of political division.

In the spring of 1834, Jesse Duncan Elliott, the commandant of the Charleston Navy Yard, ordered a figurehead for the *Constitution* of the controversial President Andrew Jackson to be sculpted by a carver named Laban Beecher. Bostonians were horrified to see a city treasure defiled by Jackson's visage. The President had vetoed a bill to recharter the Second Bank of the United States, which had adverse ramifications for Boston-based merchants.

Though the *Constitution* was under the protection of other Navy ships, on July 2, using a thunderstorm as protective cover, a 28-year-old local captain named Samuel Worthington Dewey took matters into his own hands – along with a hacksaw – and paddled out to the ship, climbed it by rope, and sawed off the top half of Jackson's face.

He made a plaster cast of the head, a gift for his friend Charles Wetherill. That cast is the current top-half of Jackson's head that visitors see in the *Constitution* Museum.

Dewey took the original to Washington, D.C., intending to present it to the president himself. He only got as far as Martin Van Buren, Jackson's vice-president, to whom he recounted his tale. Secretary of the Navy Mahlon Dickerson came into possession of the head, and it remained a family heirloom through several generations. Finally, it ended up with relations in France, was rediscovered in the 1990s, and today resides in the Museum of the City of New York, along with the body from the original carving and an imitation carving of the lower half of Jackson's head.

In 2010, a television crew from Public Television's "History Detectives" program brought to Boston a wooden fragment they believed to be the mouth and chin from the original figurehead to the *Constitution*. Paired with the museum's Wetherill plaster cast, the match was perfect.

For better or for worse, Jackson was again made whole.

# Cambridge

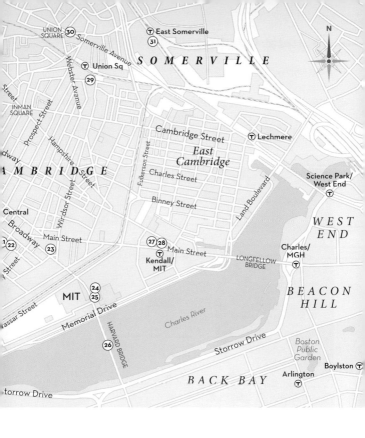

# SPHINX STATUE

*Just, calm and dignified*

*Mount Auburn Cemetery, 580 Mount Auburn Street*
*Daily 8am–5pm*
*Not easily accessible via public transport*

M any visitors to Mount Auburn Cemetery are confounded by the sculpture sitting across from the chapel: a prodigious, stoic sphinx.

Is this an ancient Egyptian artifact airlifted to New England? The grave of a famed classicist? A joke?

The author of a 1905 guidebook was nothing short of apoplectic: "In one of the most beautiful cemeteries in the United States stands today… the image of the youth-devouring female monster of the Grecian myth! Was it erected in ignorance of its meaning? Or was it an intentional insult to all our fondest hopes? Does it mean that death is like that Greek monster? What does it mean? In the Necropolis of a pagan people, to whom life and immortality had never been brought to light, that statue might not surprise us, what right has it to cumber the ground in the burial place of a Christian people?"

It is an unlikely memorial to the American Civil War. In 1872, Dr. Jacob Bigelow – who envisioned the creation of a park-like cemetery – paid sculptor Martin Milmore to carve the statue. Milmore had to do so on-site, as moving the 40-ton granite rock any substantial distance would have been challenging.

Bigelow said that the sphinx was "an ideal personification of intellect and physical force" and captured the spirit of a nation preserved. Bigelow believed that the Civil War would propel the United States toward a brighter progressive future – united and free of slavery – and would prove that the country possessed a "just, calm and dignified self-reliance."

Still, Bigelow was not entirely without racial bias: art historians have noted that he selected a Caucasian woman's head to sit atop the African lion's body.

On the front of the sphinx's base is an American water lily. On the back is an Egyptian lotus.

While the sphinx may seem an odd choice to us today – and even then stood out amid a crowded field of memorial statues featuring weary soldiers shouldering their firearms – it is reflective of a trend known as "Egyptian Revival," which saw buildings, furniture, and household items covered with Egyptian Gods and hieroglyphics.

---

Seek out the grave of inventor, futurist, and architect R. Buckminster Fuller for a peek at one of his greatest creations: a geodesic dome is carved into the headstone. Fuller was inspired by the strength of triangles in architecture (versus more typical rectangular structures.) He and his wife even resided in a "Dome Home" of Fuller's design from 1960-1971 in Carbondale, Illinois.

# THE CYMBAL ON THE GRAVE OF PUZANT H. ZILDJIAN

## *Gravesite cymbalism*

*Mount Auburn Cemetery, 580 Mount Auburn Street*
*Daily 8am-5pm*
*Green Line or Blue Line/Government Center*

The grave of Puzant H. Zildjian has an odd bit of ornamentation: there is a cymbal embedded into the stone.

Puzant, who died in 1965, was a descendant of the founder of Zildian, a percussion manufacturer that has been producing musical instruments for over 400 years. Zildjian, in fact, translates to "cymbal maker" in Armenian. The company claims the distinction of the oldest family-run company in America.

The company was started in Istanbul in 1623 by Avedis Zildjian. In 1618, Avedis created an alloy of silver, tin, and copper that proved strong, malleable, and musical, and the family has held onto the secret ever since. The Sultan's musicians adopted Avedis's cymbals for their superior quality, and, in time, the Sultan allowed Avedis to leave the palace and construct a foundry.

The business passed from generation to generation of the Zildjian family, becoming a point of pride for the region. When the company experienced a series of fires in the 1860s and the family was tempted to move the business to Paris, the Sultan of the Ottoman Empire got involved and said, "Everything necessary is done to help the Zildjian family, whose quality of cymbals is unrivaled throughout the world."

(Discrimination against Armenians would eventually see a Zildjian wrapped up in a plot to kill a later Sultan.)

In time, the Zildjian cymbal empire was destined for different shores. In 1927, Avedis III was told by his uncle it was his turn to mind the store. Avedis III, however, had moved to America in 1909 and married a local. He had established himself as a candymaker (with a specialty in bonbons) and lived in Quincy, Massachusetts. In 1929, he built a Zildian cymbal factory there, with the help of his nephew Puzant, whose grave bears the family trademark.

As jazz became more popular, Zildjian evolved its designs to keep pace, making the cymbals thinner and iterating off feedback from drummers as the company produced new types of instruments, including hi-hats. Zildjians also began producing drumsticks and mallets. The cymbals are still manufactured in Norwell, MA, and the company ranks are still filled with Zildjians.

Though Puzant never led the company himself, his grave is at least notable for signaling he went out with a bang.

# HEAD OF THE CHARLES FINISH LINE

*Row, row, row your boat*

*992 Soldiers Field Row*
*Walk along the river towards the Herter Park Amphitheatre*
*Red Line/Harvard*

Each October, over 10,000 rowers – and many thousand more spectators – descend on Boston for the largest rowing event in the world: the Head of the Charles.

Begun in 1965, the competition now stretches over three days and includes more than 60 events. The competitors hail from hundreds of universities, high schools, and extracurricular clubs, filling Harvard's historic river with their skinny sculls.

The granite and steel finish line markers, designed by Carlos Ridruejo, were installed on both sides of the Charles in 2016 as part of a beautification effort, which resulted in the creation of the Greenough Greenway on the Cambridge/Watertown bank. Before 2016, an unremarkable cement pole was the only reminder that one weekend a year the rowing world turns its eyes on Boston.

"Head" racing is a specific type of rowing competition in which athletes row the same course at slight intervals and the fastest time wins. The courses tend to be longer than traditional regatta races.

The Head of the Charles was inspired by English rowing traditions: Harvard's sculling instructor and native Brit Ernest Arlett told two of his rowers the idea, and they were off to the races.

True to its name, the Head of the Charles course covers three miles on the notoriously curvaceous Charles River. A map of the course is inscribed in the base of the finish line marker and makes clear the challenges facing any team moving at speed.

The map also highlights a second distinguishing feature of the course: the seven historic bridges it slides underneath. The bridge count, though, is controversial. Many assert there are six bridges, but fail to acknowledge that the Boston University Bridge is two separate structures: a car bridge and a train bridge. Thus, the true count is seven.

The Boston University Bridge's dual nature makes it one of only three places on earth where a boat can drive under a train, which can drive under a car, which can drive under an airplane. A local brewer, Trillium Brewing Company, honored the distinction by dubbing its quadruple IPA "Plane over Car over Train over Boat."

# ANTIOCH ROMAN MOSAIC

*A hidden Roman mosaic at Harvard*

*Harvard Business School*
*Morgan Hall*
*Inside 1st floor lobby, 15 Harvard Way*
*8am–5pm weekdays*
*Red Line/Harvard*

nside a nondescript administrative building at Harvard Business School, surrounded by a small protective moat, is a breathtaking Roman mosaic. It is easy to miss as harried graduate students rush by to make professors' office hours. It is best viewed from above: take the building's back staircase to any landing and (carefully) look down.

The artwork dates to the mid-4th century and was discovered in 1938 in the city of Antioch in today's Turkey.

Harvard and other academic institutions led archeological digs in the area. Following its discovery and removal, this mosaic remained boxed and hidden away for 30 years before being installed at the bottom of an outdoor courtyard pool at a Harvard Museum in Washington, D.C. In the 1980s, it was removed and reinstalled in Morgan Hall.

The extraordinary mosaic is an octagon stretching nearly 21 feet across and centers on the bewinged face of Tethys, the Greek goddess of fresh water and the mother of all river gods. Shouldering a rudder, Tethys is surrounded by 23 colorful sea creatures, including squid, dolphins, and a variety of bulgy-eyed fish. She is identified by name in oddly placed Greek letters.

The aquatic imagery befits Antioch, a major trading hub close to the Mediterranean Sea. Archeologists believe that this mosaic was the floor of a Roman bathhouse, and there is ongoing analysis of its stone and glass components to determine age and provenance.

# ORIGINAL WALL STREET TRADING POST

*Buying and selling in style*

*In the basement of Baker Library at 25 Harvard Way*

ounded in 1792, the New York Stock Exchange was once a modest – even sleepy – trading floor with a handful of company stocks changing hands among a small group of buyers and sellers. Prices were updated twice a day. When sales were to be made, brokers physically moved about the floor, acting on the instructions of their clientele. In 1871, with the number of traded companies growing to include railroads and insurance outfits, market makers – or so-called "specialists" – were made to sit under tall poles bearing the name of their listed stocks, thus allowing brokers to navigate an ever-busier floor more easily.

In time, both the pace and volume of sales increased, culminating in a roaring era of trade in the 1920s. Telegraphs and phones transformed the Exchange, increasing the speed of information, including the fluctuation of stock prices. In 1922, 35 miles of pneumatic tubes were installed to allow buy and sell orders to travel to relevant parties without all that walking. (The tubes' speeds were calibrated so that no trader gained an unfair advantage due to proximity to specialists.)

By 1929, the New York Stock Exchange needed greater organization than the system of poles and suction could accommodate. From 1929 to 1932, the exchange installed 17 seven foot tall, startlingly handsome horseshoe-shaped trading posts, crafted of oak, with leather seats and brass fixtures. Despite their private men's club looks, the new posts were highly functional: the upper tier created space for 100 price indicators that would change throughout the day to share the latest information, and stock specialists could run auctions between sellers and buyers more easily.

When the Exchange decided to replace the horseshoes in 1981, Harvard snapped up Post 15, which now sits neglected in the basement of Harvard Business School's largest library. Its brother, Post 13, is in the Smithsonian.

Be sure to note the post's listed stocks, some of which may look familiar: CDD (Condé Nast Publications), EK (Eastman Kodak), GOR (Goodyear Tire & Rubber Co.), and FOX (Fox Film Corp.)

# BIRTHPLACE OF ELECTRONIC SPREADSHEETS

*From in-class doodle to Excel*

*Room 108*
*HBS campus, Aldrich Hall, Soldier's Field Road, Boston*
*This is an active classroom; best chance to visit is after 3pm on a weekday*
*Red Line/Harvard*

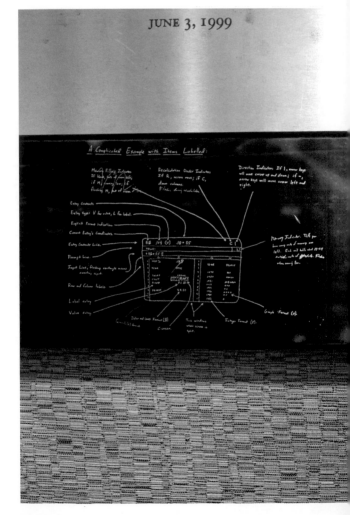

In 1978, inside Room 108 of Harvard Business School's main classroom building Aldrich Hall, MBA student Dan Bricklin had an idea for a computer program that would transform the way modern finance, business, and economies run: the electronic spreadsheet.

Bricklin recognized that, in an age of handwritten ledger books, complicated financial models required an enormous amount of wasted man hours because a change to any one input – a price, a percentage, the number of products on a shelf – required a person to recalculate and physically alter every subsequent entry. If you got one number wrong, all the work that followed would also be wrong.

While personal computers were not yet commonplace, Bricklin had studied computer science at MIT and worked on early word-processing programs. He intuited that calculation, too, could be made automated and user-friendly. Thus, sitting in his front row seat, while his classmates discussed a case study, Bricklin doodled his concept for what would become the primary driver of computer adoption among business people and a ubiquitous tool for millions.

That sketch is memorialized in brass on a plaque in Room 108 and bears a striking resemblance to its modern-day descendants – Microsoft Excel and Google Sheets.

Drawing in hand, Bricklin recruited fellow MIT alum Bob Frankston to launch Software Arts in 1979, and its groundbreaking product hit the market soon thereafter: VisiCalc, the world's first commercially available computer spreadsheet. The program was designed for the Apple II, one of the first popular mass home computer systems. While Bricklin went on to other entrepreneurial ventures, the spreadsheet program became his most famous and widely adopted product.

At the Harvard ceremony honoring his creation, Bricklin credited his father and a decidedly un-techie industry with the key insight that fueled VisiCalc: "A printer by trade, my father taught me the importance of prototyping. If you run a printing job, and it has a mistake in it, the customer won't pay. Being able to make last-minute changes is certainly a key concept in a spreadsheet."

The business world has never been the same.

# CAMBRIDGE SKATING CLUB

*A social club on ice*

*40 Willard Street*
*Not open to the general public, but the exterior and ice rink out back are the real draws*
*Red Line/Harvard*

Along Willard Street, not far from the Charles River, a charming chalet seems to have escaped Scandinavia and settled in this quiet residential neighborhood. Most days of the year, a rather forlorn sign hangs in one of its front windows: "No ice."

But that fact doesn't dampen the spirit of its delightful weathervane: look up and you'll see two graceful skaters, modeled on real Olympians

Andrée Joly and Pierre Brunet, a duo famous for developing the "shadow skating" technique of pairs mirroring each other's movements.

Founded in December 1897, the Cambridge Skating Club was born out of an intense winter-sporting controversy. Skating had long been a beloved pastime of New Englanders, and the premier spot in the Boston area was Fresh Pond (see p. 218), which even had a hotel and restaurants for ice-seeking visitors to enjoy. Thousands of skaters could fit on Fresh Pond's expanse, and the local ice-cutting business meant new fresh ice formed regularly.

In the 1880s, Fresh Pond became the centerpiece reservoir for the city's new municipal water system. Concerns about pollution led to a ban on skating on the pond along with removal of adjacent amenities and businesses. The changes sparked fierce reactions and counterreactions in the Cambridge community, with scientists divided on the pollution issue. However, by the late 1890s, skaters had lost the battle; a full ban went into effect in October 1899.

Thus, Cambridge's skaters had to take matters into their own (gloved) hands. The daughter of poet Henry Wadsworth Longfellow offered up a field she owned for the purposes of a manmade rink; today's club continues to occupy the site, just yards away from the preserved Longfellow home. The field was promptly flooded and frozen, and skating was back in session.

George H. Browne, the headmaster of the close by Browne & Nichols School (today's elite Buckingham Browne & Nichols School), became active in club leadership and professionalized the organization. Browne was an avid skater who published style and instructional manuals, and a fervent member of the "ice committee" – maintaining a daily log of the club's ice conditions.

In 1930, the club was able to buy the land and build a clubhouse in just three months' time. Architect Allen Jackson likely designed the Norwegian wooden-style building, with high gables and a tiled roof, to charm the seller of the property, Annie Longfellow Thorpe, who had married a Norwegian violinist and traveled around Norway.

© Joseph Moore

# GEORGE WASHINGTON'S PEW

*Future presidents and hidden bullet holes*

*Christ Church*
*0 Garden Street*
*Visit cccambridge.org for service times and visiting hours*
*Red Line/Harvard*

hrist Church was established in 1759 to serve colonists who
wished to keep a connection to the Church of England. Though it
was only partially finished by 1774, the church was abandoned as tensions between England and the colonies rose; most of the parishioners
were Tories who headed to Boston or back across the sea.

Soon Continental Army soldiers were lodging in Christ Church, with some itching to destroy the Loyalist stronghold. It was George and Martha Washington who stepped in to prevent its destruction; they asked to plan services in the church on 31 December 1775.

That didn't stop Washington's Colonel Palfry from delivering a political screed masquerading as a prayer, almost to the point of satire:

"Lord our Heavenly Father…we beseech Thee to look down with mercy upon his Majesty George the Third. Open his eyes and enlighten his understanding, that he may pursue the true interest of the people over whom Thou in thy Providence hast placed him. Remove far from him all wicked, corrupt men, and evil counsellors, that his throne may be established in justice and righteousness…To that end we humbly pray Thee to bless the Continental Congress…We also pray Thee to bless our provincial assemblies, magistrates, and all in subordinate places of power and trust. Be with thy servant the Commander-in-Chief of the American forces…grant that we may in due time be restored to the enjoyment of those inestimable blessings we have been deprived of by the devices of cruel and bloodthirsty men, for the sake of thy Son, Jesus Christ Our Lord. Amen."

Today there is a small plaque on the pew that the Washingtons sat in, though there is debate among historians about how active the pair were as churchgoers.

## A bullet hole in the wall

As the war ground on, the church once more became a barracks; its organ was melted for bullets. In the vestibule, behind one of the doors leading into the main body of the church, there is a bullet hole in the wall that dates to the time of the Revolution, though which side shot it and whether it was part of a military conflict or a ransacking is lost to time.

## Theodore Roosevelt at Christ Church

Washington was not the last president with a tie to Christ Church. As a Harvard student, Theodore Roosevelt served as a Sunday School teacher for three years at the church – until a strict reverend arrived who would not tolerate a Presbyterian teaching his Episcopalians. TR was told to convert or leave, and he left.

# IGOR FOKIN MEMORIAL

## *A memorial to street performers*

*1 Brattle Square, Cambridge*
*Red Line/Harvard*

The sidewalks of Brattle Square are dotted with rounded granite bollards, intended to protect pedestrians from the busy traffic just feet away. They are unfailingly boring, except for one topped by a diminutive, bright golden otherworldly creature.

The little bulgy-eyed fellow seems to have plopped down comfortably atop his perch in order to play a tune for passersby on his own flute-like nose.

This is Doo Doo, a character created by deceased popular street performer Igor Fokin who, for three years, enchanted the crowds of Harvard Square with wildly entertaining puppet shows backed by Russian folk music. Igor immigrated to the United States from the Soviet Union in 1993, with a box of handcrafted wooden marionettes in tow. Each puppet was intricately designed, carved, and dressed by Igor himself. Alongside Doo Doo were a witch, strongmen, skeletons, a jester, a swordsman, and a whimsical bird. Doo Doo's name comes from Igor's deep-voiced, Russian-accented pronunciation of "Toot toot."

Igor was trained at the Saint Petersburg Theatrical Institute, but found his career stifled by the rise of perestroika in the 1980s. With encouragement from his wife Anastasia, Igor looked for opportunities abroad. Once Igor was granted a U.S. visa as "an individual with extraordinary ability," Anastasia and their children joined him in Massachusetts. His fame and popularity grew locally and nationally; he was chosen to perform at the 1996 Atlanta Olympics. That same year, just two weeks after the birth of a new son, Igor died unexpectedly of heart failure. He was 36. Anastasia and their children returned to Russia shortly thereafter.

The street performing community of Harvard Square vowed to remember Igor. Jugglers, musicians, and other artists held benefits to help Anastasia and to raise funds for a memorial. Sculpted by fellow Russian-turned-Bostonian Konstantin Simun, the Doo Doo statue was installed in 2001 at the spot where Igor would regularly draw big crowds. Three bricks at the base of the bollard tell Igor's story and honor the art of street performance.

# CAR TALK MEMORIAL WINDOW

*Puns and pistons*

*5 John F. Kennedy Street*
*Red Line/Harvard*

Harvard Square was the unlikely home of an unlikely hit show about an unlikely topic. "Car Talk," which ran from 1977 to 2012, was a smash for National Public Radio because of the outsized personalities and delightful banter of its hosts, brothers Ray and Tom Magliozzi.

In the 1970s, the duo owned a do-it-yourself garage called Hacker's Haven. They rented out tools to non-mechanics to work on their cars, later converting it into a repair shop called the Good News Garage. In 1977, the brothers participated in a call-in auto-repair show on Boston's WBUR station, which led to a recurring segment on NPR's "Morning Edition" and, eventually, a decades-long run as the standalone show "Car Talk," which was syndicated on 660 radio stations. In 2012, the average listenership was 3.3 million a week.

The Magliozzis were known for their thick Boston accents and uproarious laughs. Despite their blue-collar sensibility, both brothers were highly educated: each held a degree from MIT and could speak to the science behind mechanical troubles. Listeners called in with all types of questions, from knocks, rattles, and bumps to how to stop wild turkeys from attacking shiny cars (camouflage vehicle covers, according to Tom and Ray.) By the finale, they had fielded 12,500 calls.

The brothers' sense of humor suffused the show, and each week's episode included a heavy dose of punning, particularly in the closing credits. Tom and Ray would list a seemingly endless cast of fictional staff, including "Creative Director Drew A. Blank," "Gas Tank Welder Stan Beck," and "Tax Consultant Lou Pole." Most famously, they were always sure to thank "Chief Legal Counsel Hugh Louis Dewey" of the law firm Dewey, Cheetham, and Howe.

The staff of "Car Talk" worked in the heart of Harvard Square, behind a third-floor window sign that proclaims it the office of "Dewey, Cheetham, and Howe." Only the most devoted of "Car Talk" lovers knows that the sign is still there, over a decade after the iconic show wrapped. The building has been redeveloped, but the owners have stated the window will be kept in place in perpetuity.

## NEARBY

### *A plaque in the shape of a 1956 Chevrolet Nomad*

At street level, just around the corner in Brattle Square, a bench bears a memorial plaque to Tom Magliozzi, who passed away in 2014. Fittingly, the plaque is in the shape of a 1956 Chevrolet Nomad, his favorite car.

# WADSWORTH HOUSE SLAVERY PLAQUE

*Home to presidents and slaves*

*1341 Massachusetts Avenue*
*Red Line/Harvard*

Just within the fence that encircles Harvard Yard stands Wadsworth House; built in 1726, it's the second oldest building on campus. Wadsworth House doesn't look like it belongs – its yellow siding clashing with the stately red brick all about it – yet it was the home of Harvard's presidents from 1726 to 1849 and hosted some of the university's most notable visitors over the years.

In the words of Harvard's former president Drew Faust, Wadsworth House "was George Washington's initial headquarters when he came to take command of the Continental Army in 1775. Ralph Waldo Emerson boarded in the house when he was a student. Andrew Jackson held a reception of students in the house in 1833 after he received his

honorary degree. Later in the century, Henry Adams lived here as an assistant professor."

But Wadsworth House is also tied up with some of Harvard's hidden history, which has only just begun to come to light: the university's entanglement with slavery. From church and town records, personal papers, and university faculty minutes, it is known that Harvard presidents Benjamin Wadsworth (who served 1725–1737) and Edward Holyoke (1737–1769) each kept slaves during their years in Wadsworth House.

The names of four of the enslaved are known and recognized on a plaque on the house, just within the Harvard gates – Titus, Venus, Bilhah, Juba. At the unveiling of the plaques, Faust noted, "We name the names to remember these stolen lives."

Harvard, along with many American universities, is investing heavily in researching historic ties to slavery and changing names and symbols accordingly. In 2016, following protests, Harvard Law School replaced its official seal, which formerly featured three sheaves of wheat, an allusion to the family crest of Isaac Royall Jr., Massachusetts's largest slaveholder at the time. Royall used his wealth to endow Harvard's first law professorship. (see p. 242)

### The oldest surviving headstone of a Black person in the Americas

Just across from Harvard Yard on Garden Street is Cambridge's Old Burying Ground, home to what is believed to be the oldest surviving headstone of a Black person in the Americas. It reads, "Here lyes the body of Cicely, Negro, late Servant to the Reverend Minister William Brattle; she died April 8, 1714. Being 15 years old."

# SCHOOL PENNANTS PRESERVED IN TILE

*Fast food and hidden mosaics*

*1326 Massachusetts Avenue, Cambridge*
*Red Line/Harvard*

The Waldorf Lunch System opened at this site in 1913.

The custom tile work and pennants you see here were uncovered by our demo team. We're indebted to our construction team (Justin Kelly Contracting) who painstakingly protected and restored this unique piece of Harvard history.

The Waldorf Lunch System was a "lunch place," what we might now call a fast casual restaurant. The "system" grew to nearly 200 units at its peak and served as one of the first prototype restaurant chains in the world.

When the Waldorf Lunch opened, Harvard Square was a different place. The subway had just been completed March of the same year. Cambridge housed factories. This cafeteria was a crossroads for day laborers and poets and students.

In 2016, when Clover – a vegetarian fast-food chain founded by an MIT and Harvard graduate – was looking to move into a new location in Harvard Square, the company selected a corner storefront that had last been home to an unassuming Chinese restaurant. When a crew began demolition to ready the space for renovation, the workers discovered that behind the plain, modern walls was an 100-year-old original tile artwork celebrating the space's connection to Harvard University and America's other great academic institutions.

Clover's founder Ayr Muir, a history lover, spearheaded the restoration of the tiles, which can be enjoyed by visitors to the restaurant today.

The tiles were originally the decor of the Waldorf Lunch – a predecessor to modern fast-food chains and a New England icon of its time. The Harvard Square location opened in 1913, focused on serving the local student population and factory workers.

The uppermost portion of the wall features a long line of glass pennants bearing the names and colors of 38 elite schools, familiar and not. The Ivy League and Seven Sister universities are joined by MIT – simply called "Tech" – as well as a bevy of New England liberal arts colleges like Bowdoin and Holy Cross, ritzy private high schools like Andover and Exeter, and a handful of now-defunct institutions.

The "Carlisle" flag refers to the Carlisle Indian Industrial School, an experimental state-run Native American boarding school that closed its doors in 1918 after 39 years of operation. At its height, Carlisle's football team was a powerhouse and fierce rival of the Harvard Crimson. Football historians today credit Carlisle's team with the creation of the overhand spiral throw and the fake handoff.

Boston College is notably missing: the original was mysteriously pried loose before the modern restoration. In its place, Muir created a replacement pennant reading "Full Circle" – the name of a small independent elementary school that his parents ran in Western Massachusetts.

The walls also feature a mosaic of repeating crimson Hs, and don't overlook the floor: what first appears to be a maze-like rectilinear design is in fact a clever series of interlocking Hs, another nod to the university just outside the door.

# THE PIG HEAD
# AT THE PORCELLIAN CLUB

*Pig gate and its mate*

*1324 Massachusetts Avenue*
*Red Line/Harvard*

At 1324 Massachusetts Avenue, there is a locked door. Above it, a pig's head is carved into the keystone. Don't knock! For this is the headquarters of the Porcellian Club, Harvard's most exclusive secret society.

Among the university set, these groups are referred to as "finals clubs." As the ornamentation suggests, the club's name derives from the Latin *porcus* – meaning pig – and honors its founding myth, a group of students enjoying a roasted pig feast in a small and presumably pungent dorm room. Locals call it "The Porc" for short.

The membership is exclusively male – a subject of controversy over the last decade – and has a reputation for snobbiness. Non-members are only permitted to enter a small room on the first floor, known as the "Bike Room." The upper floors are rumored to evoke a traditional, stuffy, wood-paneled British-inflected men's club, complete with billiard tables and dusty bookshelves.

Though Porcellian members are tight-lipped about their rituals, they seem to center mostly on shared meals, singing club songs, and venerating historical artifacts that are littered about the clubhouse, many featuring the trademark boar.

Theodore Roosevelt was a member, as was Supreme Court Justice Oliver Wendell Holmes Jr., Senator and Representative Henry Cabot Lodge, and the Winklevoss twins, of Facebook lawsuit fame. As an undergraduate, Franklin Delano Roosevelt longed to be invited (at Harvard they say "punched") but was blackballed and had to make do with membership in The Fly, a rival club.

## NEARBY
### The Pig Head on the McKean Gate

Standing outside the front door, look across Massachusetts Avenue at the gate into Harvard Yard. That is the McKean Gate – it, too, is topped by the head of a pig (and this one seems to stare back rather more aggressively than the first). The gate honors Joseph McKean, who, in 1791, founded The Porcellian by hosting that first pig dinner. The initial dinner party attendees called themselves the Argonauts, then eventually The Pig Club. The name only later took on its distinctly snooty Latin-bent. Look closely and you'll see the initials "PC" are hidden in the McKean Gate's ironwork, a permanent callout to McKean's legacy just across the street.

# THE TINY STATUES
# OF PETER J. SOLOMON GATE

*Academic Wonderland*

*Quincy Street and Harvard Street*
*Red Line/Harvard*

While Harvard Yard is surrounded by an imposing iron fence, 25 historic gates – ranging in design from the grand to the pedestrian – allow entry to students, tourists, and intellectual luminaries.

Each gate tells a story through its iconography, often dictated by its funder. Sharp-eyed visitors will note the self-aggrandizement of rich alumni, the memorialization of Harvard presidents, and the religious roots of a college originally created to educate ministers.

Only one gate, though, honors "Alice in Wonderland." Installed in 2020, the construction of the portal – technically known as the Peter J. Solomon Gate – was part of a donation to renovate the Houghton Library, home to rare books and manuscripts. Solomon also donated a large collection of historic children's literature, including an extremely rare first edition of "Alice's Adventures in Wonderland," which was recalled after its first printing.

The Gate's design is shockingly playful in the staid university setting. The designer, Eric Höweler, hid tiny statues and carvings depicting characters from "Alice" – a running white rabbit, a pocket watch, the Queen of Heart's crown, the Mad Hatter's signature top hat, an unmistakable Cheshire Cat.

The stone pillars on either side of the gate feature a hidden silhouette of Peter Rabbit, another treasured character in Solomon's collection. (Be patient: it can take a moment to see the inflection points in the tall ears. The deepest indentation denotes Peter's face.).

Höweler drew inspiration from Lewis Carroll and Beatrix Potter. "Both stories contain themes of adventure and curiosity, mischief and the marvelous. Peter [Solomon] was looking for an element of whimsy – reflecting on his time at Harvard, he talked about how he cherished the world of ideas that the University opened up and how he wanted to encourage students to be curious and not take themselves too seriously."

# FORBES PIGMENT COLLECTION

*A hidden indoor rainbow*

4th floor of 32 Quincy Street
Tuesday–Sunday 10am–5pm
Red Line/Harvard

Harvard is home to the Forbes Pigment Collection, a library of 2,700 historic pigment specimens that today are used by art historians and preservationists for scientific study and art conservation. It is one of the largest such collections in the world.

Visitors can only glimpse the riot of colors from a distance – across an open-air atrium – but it's worth it: rows and rows of oddly shaped beakers and bottles, shelves of jars of varying sizes – all sealed tight, many with yellowing typewritten labels – create a shocking effect: a hidden indoor rainbow.

The collection is named for its founder, Edward Waldo Forbes, who served as Director of the university's Fogg Museum from 1909 to 1944 and created a Department of Conservation and Technical Research in 1928. Forbes was a collector himself and a pioneer in employing science to illuminate – and save – works of art. Forbes believed that understanding an artwork meant understanding the materials and techniques that made it, plus the effects of time, light exposure, wear, and chemistry. Thus, he began to accrue not only paintings, but pigments, dyes, powders, resins, paints, and inks from around the world as reference materials.

The stories of historic pigment production astound: ancient Phoenicians had to grind up 250,000 murex snail shells to create half an ounce of the color Tyrian purple, which the Romans used to distinguish the to-

gas of high-status individuals. Bone black was made from burned bones, horns, and tusks. Even grislier, in 17th century Europe, mummy brown was made by grinding the remains of ancient Egyptian mummies.

Lead white is a strikingly bright white that is also highly toxic. Dutch pigment makers would stack pots of vinegar and lead, then cover them with manure to cause the evaporation of acetic acid and carbon dioxide. Three months later, despite the smell, they had the lead carbonate they needed.

In medieval Europe, dragon blood red was believed to be the dried blood resulting from an epic battle between dragons and elephants. While it's an exciting myth, the pigment is actually produced from dracorubin, a compound produced by trees in South America, Southeast Asia, and elsewhere.

The collection continues to grow: in 2020, the museum acquired 20 pigments used by Georgia O'Keeffe, each with a handwritten label by the artist herself.

Forbes also built the university's first lab dedicated to art, recruiting Harvard chemistry professor Rutherford John Gettens to join the museum. Gettens's legacy lives on: next to the Forbes Collection is a narrow cabinet holding the Gettens Collection of Binding Media and Varnishes, a fine (if less colorful) complement to the pigments. Today, the Harvard Art Museum's analytical laboratory – the descendant of Gettens's original – sits just behind these cabinets so researchers can have ready access to their incomparable treasures.

> While visitors cannot get up close to the pigments, Harvard has created an excellent free audio tour at harvardartmuseums.org/tour/660

# DEWEY DECIMAL MURALS

*All the world's knowledge in four paintings*

*Cambridge Public Library – Reading Room and Delivery Room*
*449 Broadway*
*Monday–Thursday 9am–9pm, Saturday 9am–5pm, Sundays 1pm–5pm*
*(September to June)*
*Red Line/Harvard*

The Cambridge Public Library is overshadowed as a tourist spot by its big brother across the river, the Boston Public Library, which is awash with showy statues and grand murals. But in the historic wing of the original Cambridge Public Library building, the Reading Room and

Delivery Room (now a computer lab) are home to four grand murals that pay tribute to the organizational prowess of the Dewey Decimal system and the global history of the written word.

The murals were commissioned in 1934 by the Civil Works Administration, a Depression-era federal job creation program. Artists Elizabeth Tracy – a local Radcliffe alumna – and Arthur Willis Oakman drew on the Dewey Decimal System's 10 classifications of knowledge: General Works, Philosophy, Religion, Sociology, Philology (spot the Tower of Babel), Literature, History, Fine Arts, Pure Science, and – as the mural would have it – "Useful Arts."

The remaining murals illustrate "The History of Books and Paper" and "The Development of the Printing Press."

In chronological order, the paintings recognize achievements by Babylonians, Egyptians, Chinese, Greeks, Romans, hardworking Italian monks, and medieval British knights.

The printing press is traced from Gutenberg's press to mechanized printing. Don't overlook William Caxton – the first English printer – paying tribute to his patroness, the notably haughty Duchess of Burgundy. Tucked beneath his arm is a copy of the first book printed in English – *Recuyell of the Historyes of Troy* – ready to be presented to the duchess, a moment so heavy with drama even the court jester has dropped to his knees.

Tracy and Oakman also didn't pass up a chance at hometown pride: a middle panel celebrates Stephen Daye, who brought the first printing press to America in 1639.

Also in the Cambridge Public Library, adjacent to the Delivery Room, don't miss the monumentally large inscription of the Ten Commandments and admonishment "Men, Women, Children: if you obey these Commandments you will be happy. If you disobey them sorrow will come upon you." These threatening words have proven controversial among today's liberal Cambridge population, but the 1887 inscriptions were a condition of the land and construction of the library by its deeply religious benefactor Frederick Rindge.

# COLLECTION OF HISTORICAL SCIENTIFIC INSTRUMENTS

*Brain molds and a cyclotron*

*Harvard Science Center*
*1 Oxford Street*
*Sunday–Friday 11am–4pm*
*Red Line/Harvard*

Tucked in an unloved corner of the Harvard Science Center – which was built to look like a camera out of respect to its funder, Polaroid inventor Edwin Land – the university's Collection of Historical Scientific Instruments is a small gallery of treasures and oddities.

While Harvard was collecting useful and beautiful scientific instruments since its founding, the collection wasn't formally consolidated until 1948. Today, it accounts for 20,000 objects dating from 1400 to the present and spans scientific fields.

Many of the older objects are as much art pieces as scientific implements. America's pre-eminent colonial stargazer was John Winthrop, and his collection of polished brass telescopes, with ivory handles and delicately scrolled feet, might convince you that astronomy was a more refined profession in the 1700s. (Winthrop was the only person in North America to observe the Transit of Venus in 1761.) A majestic 12-sided mahogany "grand orrery" – that is, model solar system – boasts 12 decorative brass figures of Ben Franklin, Isaac Newton, and James Bowdoin (a former Massachusetts governor), cast by none other than revolutionary Paul Revere. A hand-crank and complex gear system make the planets and their moons revolve, viewable through a large glass dome.

The collection takes a turn for the macabre in its exhibits on biology and physiology. A foursome of wax anatomical models from 1890 shows the brains of an alligator, pigeon, rabbit, and dog. Two other models seem to show a run-of-the-mill orangutan and a slightly depressed human fetus, until you note the right side of their skulls have been removed to reveal the inner workings. An overlarge plaster ear and papier mâché eye take it all in from behind glass. Look closely and you'll see these are so-called "clastic" models. They can be cleverly disassembled and were used to teach anatomy to 19th century students.

# BLASCHKA GLASS MARINE MODELS

*Menagerie of sea life*

*Harvard Natural History Museum*
*26 Oxford Street*
*Monday–Sunday 9am–5pm*
*Red Line/Harvard*

Jelly
*Catostylus tagi*
Cnidaria–Scyphozoa–Rhizostomeae
MCZ SC#14B  Crambessa tagi

The Harvard Natural History Museum has a popular gallery devoted to a collection of glass flowers created by expert glass modelers Leopold and Rudolf Blaschka. Often overlooked but equal in precision – and perhaps greater in beauty – is a smaller collection of glass sea creatures that the Blaschkas made for private collectors, teaching institutions, and museums in the late 1800s.

Harvard's collection tops 430 models of invertebrate sea creatures, a rotating subset of which are on display. For decades they were used in classrooms as hands-on teaching tools because real animals were difficult to preserve. The glass models were eventually relegated to storage for nearly 100 years, many growing dull or breaking. In 2005, the Museum of Comparative Zoology undertook a major effort to restore them.

Out of their workshop in Dresden, Germany, the father-son Blaschka team aspired to anatomical accuracy, and the models glow with life: squid with whip-like tentacles, octopus, sea slugs, jellyfish, marine worms, anemones. Leopold Blaschka became fascinated with the glass-like look of marine life on a boat trip near the Azores, writing "[w]e look out over the darkness of the sea, which is as smooth as a mirror; there emerges all around in various places a flashlike bundle of light beams, as if it is surrounded by thousands of sparks, that form true bundles of fire." He was hooked.

The Blaschkas manufactured an astounding 630 different glass invertebrates model types. They designed from living models, specimens preserved in alcohol, sketches, and art in textbooks – which sometimes led to misjudgments in scale and dimension. In the mid-1800s, home aquariums were becoming common, and many people purchased and submerged Blaschka models in place of real animals to save on cost and maintenance. Teaching institutions and museums used the models in place of preserved specimens, which collapsed and faded in color.

Daisy Anemone
Cereus pedunculatus
Cnidaria-Anthozoa-Actiniaria

Sadly, when Harvard hired the pair to exclusively produce glass flower models, they abandoned animal modeling.

Take time to swing by the flower collection, too, as you'll get to see a small box of glass eyes the Blaschkas designed for human prosthetics and animal taxidermy.

# HARVARD'S RESIDENT RHINOS

*The world's fauna preserved*

*Harvard Bio Labs Building*
*16 Divinity Ave*
*The building entrance and courtyard are tucked off to the right where Divinity Avenue dead ends*
*Red Line/Harvard*

**A**mong Harvard University's hundreds of sedate red-brick buildings, in a lovely, secluded little corner of the campus that few who aren't associated with the labs would think to visit, sit two sculptures of enormous female specimens of *Rhinoceros unicornis*.

Dubbed Bessie and Victoria in honor of the English Queens, the bronze statues were commissioned in 1930 by Harvard President A. Law-

rence Lowell, who is today remembered not for whimsy but for a long record of racism, homophobia, antisemitism, and sexism. Nonetheless, it was Lowell who hired 30-year-old Katharine Lane Weems, one of America's first celebrated female sculptors, to design the exterior of the labs.

Weems specialized in animal sculpture, perfected through close observation of live specimens. Bessie and Victoria were modeled on a female rhino at the Bronx Zoo and are morphologically accurate, down to each wrinkle, joint, and muscle. Weems scaled both statues up to match the largest recorded specimen of the species. Each statue weighs in at a dainty three tons.

## Pranking the rhinos

The official unveiling was on 12 May 1937. As the curtains were pulled back, it was revealed some playful students had slipped a bedpan under each, starting a long tradition of pranking Bessie and Victoria. If you visit at Halloween, you may catch one or both in costume. Otherwise, keep an eye out for painted toenails or piles of clay fashioned to resemble rhino poop.

## An ornate door and a 400-foot-long frieze of 30 animals

While the rhinos tend to get the most attention, they are just one piece of Weems's three-part decorative scheme. The ornate doors to the Bio Labs feature 24 bronze panels depicting creatures of sea, air, and land. The mosquito is a particularly lively contribution.

Finally, near the top exterior of the Bio Labs, Weems used a pneumatic drill to carve a 400 foot long frieze of 30 animals from across the world's four major climate zones: polar, temperate, equatorial, and marine. The menagerie includes an enormous group of African elephants, prowling tigers, beefy bison, flying pelicans, a giant anteater, and a smiling tapir fit for a Disney cartoon.

Weems also sculpted "Dolphins of the Sea" outside the New England Aquarium in downtown Boston and donated 30 bronze animal sculptures to the Boston Museum of Science.

# JULIA CHILD'S SIGNATURE

*A sign-off in cement*

92 Kirkland Street
Red Line/Harvard

Julia Child transformed the American palate with her breakthrough cookbook, "Mastering the Art of French Cooking," and multiple TV series that transformed her into an icon. For 40 years, she lived in Cambridge at 103 Irving Street and shot many of her big-hearted cooking lessons out of her home kitchen. Sadly for the people of Boston, in 2001 Julia donated that kitchen – cabinets, appliances, counters, tools – to the Smithsonian Museum. It was dismantled and moved to Washington, D.C.

In 1990, Julia donated her home and office to her alma mater, Smith College in Northampton, MA, but retained the right to live there. When she relocated to a retirement community in 2001, Smith sold the home for $2.35 million and used the funds to build a campus center – which in 2022 the school said would be named in her honor. The school also celebrates a Julia Child Day the Thursday before Thanksgiving each year, adding signature French dishes to its cafeteria offerings.

While 103 Irving still stands, it is a private residence and closed to the public. However, Julia did leave a hidden mark for her hometown to remember her by, as thanks to a local grocer.

Butcher Jack Savenor kept Julia supplied with the high-quality ingredients and cuts of meat that were considered radical to the cooking American public at the time. He was an occasional guest on the show. Savenor's Butcher Shop and Market still stands (or rather, stands again after a fire in 1992) and just outside its doors Julia scrawled her initials and signature sign-off – "Bon appetit" – into the sidewalk's wet cement.

It's virtually the only remaining memorial in town for one of Boston's most famous residents.

Harvard's Schlesinger Library has one of the world's finest collections of historic cookbooks at about 20,000 volumes. Among its treasures are the papers of Julia Child and her husband, Paul. The Schlesinger Library resides on the former Radcliffe campus and the cookbook collection was moved to the school in the 1960s from Harvard's Widener Library because the university thought the content was more fitting for a female audience. Radcliffe's feminists didn't love the implication, but today the collection is a source of great pride. The library is open to the public and features rotating exhibitions, often themed around the history of women.

# COSMIC MOOSE AND BEARS VILLE

*Good fence, good vibes*

*37 Brookline Street*
*Red Line/Central*

It's hard to say what will catch your attention first. It may be the spooky boarded-up triple-decker house. It might be the strange angle of the house to the street, as if it were haphazardly yanked 45 degrees sideways. It could be the enormous, irregular purple fence that surrounds the house, covered in hundreds of scribbled sayings and bits of wisdom, smatterings of fluorescent green-yellow-pink paint, and random wooden sculptures and bric-a-brac nailed in place, maybe yesterday or maybe 30 years ago.

It will probably be the big black silhouettes of a bull moose and stubby-legged bear.

The house is known as Cosmic Moose and Bears Ville, home to artist-cum-mystic Peter Valentine from 1991 to his death in 2022. The fence was Peter's life's work, his canvas for sharing with passersby quasi-religious musings on life, silly bits of nonsense, and advertisements for lessons in "electromagnetic martial arts."

Peter described it to SPACES Archives as "a living energy which evokes the viewers' divine essence from their deep cosmic self."

It can be difficult to pick favorites from the infinite layers of overlapping writing accumulated over decades, but here are a few standouts of Peter's folk wisdom:

"Problems aren't the problem / Solving them Magnificently, is the problem."

"Words and clothes are the best of lovers."

"This is the greatest thought that has ever or will ever be thunk. It is, 'there are no students, only Teachers.'"

And sing-song silliness: "Body speakers/Twilight tweakers" and "Movie actor Chiropractor".

How Peter, who was believed to live off a small government subsidy, came into possession of the house is the stuff of legend. As the story goes, in the 1980s, MIT sought to expand into an area called Cambridgeport, which required the rehousing of residents. Peter was one of the holdouts, claiming he couldn't leave his rent-controlled apartment because it was "in karma" with his cosmic energy. To entice him to leave, MIT reportedly gave him the triple-decker and offered to reposition it so his energy fields could remain intact.

Recent journalism suggests that Peter may have in fact paid some amount to MIT, though the truth will likely be lost to time: the artist died in August 2022.

But his fence, home, and the Moose and Bear still stand as testaments to Peter's unique outlook on the cosmos.

# COOKIE MEDALLIONS

## 22

*Sweet apartments*

*129 Franklin Street*
*Red Line/Central*

The early to mid-20th century was a boom time for small candy manufacturers in the Boston area. Drivers on I-93 passing Charlestown can still see the wacky sign for Schrafft's, the company credited with introducing jellybeans to an American audience, even though it shut its doors in 1981.

Marshmallow fluff was invented in Somerville in 1917 by a door-to-door sweet peddler. Cambridge had so many sweet makers – according to the Cambridge Historical Society as many as 66 by 1946 – that Main Street was known as "Confectioner's Row." Charleston Chews were invented there.

Much of this history is lost, but a few artifacts remain. The New England Confectionary Company   makers of chalky Necco wafers – operated here from 1927 to 2003. In 1999, it bought out and shut down a century-old outfit called Squirrel Brand Co., which specialized in taffies and nougats; the Squirrel Brand Co. sign still can be seen on the side of its factory at 12 Boardman Street.

While nondescript from the outside, the factory at 810 Main Street is owned by Tootsie Roll and churns out 15 million Junior Mints daily.

And though it has moved on from its candy-making past, the owners at 129 Franklin Street have hidden a nod to that history in their architecture. The Kennedy Biscuit Lofts occupy the building that was once the headquarters of Kennedy Biscuits, inventors of the Fig Newton. Fig Newtons make obvious their local ties: they are named for the nearby town of Newton – a naming convention the company also applied to several less popular products, including Harvards, Beacon Hills, and Shrewsburys.

After joining forces with other bakeries, Kennedy Biscuits rebranded as the National Biscuit Company, or more familiarly as Nabisco. Nabisco, creator of Oreos, also had hits with the Lorna Doone – a shortbread cookie – and Ritz Crackers, Teddy Grahams, and Chips Ahoy.

While the factory was converted into residences, the brick columns out front are inset with medallions in the shapes of the company's trademark treats, including Social Tea and 5 O'Clock Tea Biscuits, Triton cookies, and Arrowroots.

# TECH MODEL RAILROAD CLUB

## 23

*Toy trains, real software*

*Room N52–118*
*265 Massachusetts Avenue*
*Visit tmrc.mit.edu/ for upcoming openings or to arrange a tour*
*Red Line/Central*

The Tech Model Railroad Club is famous to people who fall within two very well-defined groups: model train enthusiasts and computer software historians. The relationship between the two, while not obvious at first, becomes clear once one has seen how the MITers' model railroad works, backed as it is by student-created software and an extensive network of sensors tracking and organizing what's happening on the rails.

A visit to the TMRC (pronounced TUH-murk) is also a standout way to experience the uniquely MIT attitude of being both shockingly brilliant and cheekily flippant about rule-following.

Founded in 1946, the club's extensive railroad set-up has only been moved once. The club's first home was in a legendary building on campus, Building 20, which was intended to be a temporary home to MIT's military research during World War II. It remained in place for 55 years, gaining the nickname the "Plywood Palace" and a reputation that students could basically do whatever they wanted within its walls. The rogue spirit engendered by Building 20 remains a proud part of the TMRC culture.

TMRC moved to its current home in 1997. In the ensuing decades, members have built an extensive network of cityscapes, residential areas, parks, foliage, cars, trucks, underpasses, and many colorful pedestrians. There are miles and miles of track, a roundhouse, and a freight yard.

Particularly notable is a tall model building with many windows, which is based on MIT's real-world Green Building; the model is programmed to light-up and emulate a game of Tetris, including the video game's tinny music. (A group of students once wired the real 18-story building to do the same thing.)

The trains are electrically powered through the rails and the whole system is run by "System 3," a third-generation software program created by MIT students themselves. The system can automatically throw switches and turn power on and off to specific tracks, allowing many trains to run at once with no human intervention.

The history of TMRC is tied closely to the broader "hacker culture" among software engineers; early members are credited with inventing the concept that "information wants to be free" – a core belief among hacker zealots.

# "BARS WITH COLORS WITHIN SQUARES" BY SOL LEWITT

## 24

*A secret geometric oasis*

MIT
*Enter 77 Massachusetts Avenue and walk straight down a very long hallway
(called "The Infinite" by MITers). Take a right at the end of the hallway and then
another immediate right. The artwork can be seen through a door straight ahead
Monday–Friday 6am–7pm
Red Line/Kendall-MIT*

**M**IT's classroom buildings can have a Hogwartsian feel: as the institute has grown, building after building has been connected via unlikely stairs, tunnels, and passageways. It is so easy to lose one's way; the students have created a website – whereis.mit.edu – as a navigational aid.

As the spaces grow more boxed in, shadowy piazzas and nooks abound. But one such atrium – U-shaped and spanning 5,500 square feet – explodes with color. The floor, designed by modernist American artist Sol LeWitt, has a name that is deceptive for its forthrightness: "Bars of Colors within Squares." The fifteen 18 foot by 18 foot squares hum with vibrant colors and sharp geometric shapes.

The artwork encircles Building 6C, a handsome glass structure built in the middle of a former courtyard. Raised glass-encased bridges span the spaces above, connecting 6C to other buildings in the Physics complex and giving LeWitt's eye-popping colors a distinctly futuristic edge.

The squares themselves are mesmerizing, rewarding close study from multiple perspectives, including from above. Changes in light, too, alter the colorful scenes. From one viewpoint, a jumble of trapezoids resolves into letters of the alphabet. From another, visual tricks create depth and height; primary color staircases seem to lead to a mystical portal below. A border of white and gray outlines each square, giving the sense of a children's book at a massive scale, laid out page by page.

The floors are made of terrazzo, an unusual mix of epoxy resin and beads made of recycled glass in order to achieve the requisite brightness. Sadly, LeWitt himself never saw the floor – he died just days before his designs became reality in 2007.

Besides the wonderful visuals, visitors to this secret hideaway are struck by the utter quiet of this far reach of the MIT universe. With machines, students, and faculty incessantly whirring about the hallways of this world-famous science university, it is ironic a place devoted to art provides the campus's most peaceful sanctuary.

# HART NAUTICAL GALLERY

*World's greatest mini shipyard*

55 Massachusetts Avenue
Monday–Friday 6am–7pm
Red Line/Kendall-MIT

**M**IT has a long and underappreciated connection to the sea. A Department of Naval Architecture was established in 1893, with a focus on ship construction. In 1901, at the government's request, the school offered courses exclusively for boat builders for the U.S. Navy. Later, a workshop was built so students could create half-models from blueprints. During World War I, the school provided a series of intensive courses in ship design to support the Navy's war effort.

From this early start, MIT's research grew to encompass countless topics related to the ocean, commerce, and war: ship design and building, the business of shipping, marine electrical engineering, propulsion engineering. In 1971, the discipline was renamed "Oceanic Engineering" to encapsulate its breadth. In 1976, the institute was named a Sea Grant College, an exclusive program funded by the U.S. Department of Commerce's National Oceanic and Atmospheric Administration to support the development of marine resources.

There are markers of this nautical legacy sprinkled around campus. Note the two giant anchors flanking the (locked) entrance to Building 5 at 55 Massachusetts Avenue. Just up the road is MIT's main entrance at 77 Massachusetts Avenue; enter there and take a right. You will find an extraordinary (and extraordinarily quiet) gallery of model boats – a small portion of MIT's Hart Nautical Collections. These are what remains of the Institute's former Nautical Museum, founded in 1921 and later merged with the MIT Museum.

The collection is one of the most extensive of its kind and encompasses 1,500 ship models, navigational instruments, and historic designs for ships, as well as thousands of photos, films, and business records.

The models on display range from tall ships to famous historical re-creations (the *Mayflower*, the *Susan Constant*) to American Cup-winning yachts. A 1591 Korean Turtle warship has decks topped with iron spikes to prevent unwelcome boarding. An 1880 "Zulu" Scottish fishing vessel (named during the Zulu War by Scots who sympathized with the Zulus as victims of British aggression) has a label that teases, "Although it can now be seen only with the aid of a dental mirror, the cabin is fully fitted with bunks complete with bedding."

# SMOOT MARKS
# ON THE HARVARD BRIDGE

*The measure of a man*

*The bridge stretches from Cambridge to Boston across from 182 Memorial Drive*
*Red Line/Kendall-MIT*

The name of Harvard Bridge has caused much controversy, as it sits squarely within MIT's campus, it is miles (and many bridges) away from the Harvard campus, and a healthy rivalry exists between the two elite schools.

When the bridge was constructed in 1891, though, MIT's campus was across the river in the city of Boston, so it made perfect sense to name it in honor of Cambridge's leading institution. Thus, if you hear locals referencing "the MIT Bridge" or, more diplomatically, "the Mass Ave Bridge," know it is all the same landmark.

It was an MIT undergraduate, however, who left the biggest mark on the history of the Harvard Bridge, quite literally. In October 1958, Oliver Smoot was a freshman hoping to join the Lambda Chi Alpha Fraternity. As one of their pledging activities, Oliver and his fellow would-be frat brothers were assigned to measure and mark the .4-mile bridge in an original unit of measurement: the Smoot. The Smoot was defined as the height of young Oliver – 5 feet 7 inches.

A small group accompanied Oliver and dutifully marked the entirety of the Harvard Bridge using chalk and paint. The length of the bridge was determined to be "364.4 plus-or-minus one ear." Oliver has recounted that the prank took its toll: he originally intended to do a push-up at each interval but quickly realized the strain of simply laying down and getting up over 300 times was strenuous enough.

As you walk the bridge today, note the tic marks indicating each Smoot, with a number for each group of ten.

The Smoot has developed a cult following: Google Search will convert any measurement to Smoots on request and it was accepted as a defined measure by the American Heritage Dictionary in 2011. In 2008, on the 50th anniversary of his nighttime escapade, a plaque honoring Oliver Smoot was installed on the bridge's Cambridge side.

In a novelistic turn, later in life Oliver went on to serve as the chairman of the American National Standards Institute and the President of the International Organization for Standardization, the very bodies that set standards of measurement and compatibility for worldwide commerce and industry.

Every other year, the Lambda Chi Alpha pledges refresh the paint in honor of their brother.

# KENDALL SQUARE ROOF GARDEN ㉗

## *A parking garage garden*

*325 Main Street; enter the parking garage and select "R"*
*Red Line/Kendall-MIT*

As both the heart of MIT and the center of the American biotech industry, the streets of Kendall Square teem with distracted engineers, stressed out office workers, and all manner of academics. Amid the chaos, a nondescript parking garage is home to a secret rooftop garden, complete with city views and walking paths.

The Kendall Square Roof Garden is unique among Boston public gardens in that it remains green year-round, despite harsh New England winters: the space is covered in 7,000 square feet of turf, not real grass. In the warmer months, though, nature dominates; the garden is home to seasonal flowers including tulips and roses, plus a handful of not insubstantial trees, considering that they're four stories up and growing on a ceiling.

The current iteration of the park atop the parking garage is the third; the move of several leading companies into the Square spurred a broader rethink of the park area – particularly because the new construction changed the plot's exposure to the sun.

The space was designed by Boston-area firm Lemon Brooke. Reflecting on the park's five-year planning and building process, codesigner Christian Lemon said, "Technically, it's one of the most complex gardens you'll find." The turf – officially an artificial grass called SynLawn – is much more common in California, and convincing cynical New Englanders to accept it has been an ongoing process. The reality is that no grassy lawn could sustain itself given the amount of shade in this urban nook.

Despite its synthetic covering, the landscape is naturalistic, with gentle rises and slopes contrasting cannily with the adjacent techy office buildings. The landscape architects opted for native species that could grow in the unique elevated environment and thrive despite limited access to the sun. Still, there are distinctly non-Massachusetts flora that have caused some controversy, not least the tall bamboo used to cover certain views of the parking lot.

Lemon Brooke's team added a number of amenities that make this hidden garden feel more like a home: "We thought of it as an outdoor living room." Indeed, there is a shaded terrace with a rentable outdoor kitchen, a play area (currently a pickleball court), an outdoor movie screen, and raised community garden plots.

# "KENDALL BAND"

## *Subway made sonic*

## 28

*Kendall Square T Station, 300 Main Street*
*Red Line/Kendall*

From 1986 to 1988, Paul Matisse – the grandson of Henri Matisse and the stepson of Marcel Duchamp – installed a three-part musical art piece between the inbound and outbound tracks of the Boston T at Kendall Square.

The piece – called "Kendall Band" – consists of Pythagoras, a series of mallets and 16 aluminum chimes; Kepler, a suspended 55-inch metal ring and hammer; and Galileo, a large metal sheet that rumbles and shakes. Separately, their music breaks up a workaday commute. Together, they make a bit of a racket.

The instruments are controlled by handles that are installed on both platforms and allow subway riders to transfer energy into the devices. The hammers swing slowly and build momentum before they actually make contact with the instruments. Once they do, the effects last: Kepler resonates for a full five minutes, whether platform dwellers want it to or not.

The musical sculptures have proven fragile over the years, with their various gears, wires, and hinges falling into disrepair due to use and trying conditions, not least hundreds of train cars a day speeding past on both sides. Matisse himself was charged with repairing the piece, and spent two decades doing so, always leaving a handwritten note on the platform. Platform dwellers would invariably leave him notes, both encouraging and otherwise:

"If you spent my tax $ on this then may you DIE SLOWLY."

"Try to get a taper connection from the first vertical to the second on this side and an oversized second vertical linkage with perhaps an internal shock absorber." (Remember: this is the T stop for MIT engineers.)

In 2009, a passenger, disappointed to find the Kendall Band yet again broken, reached out to MIT to recruit helpers who might maintain the historic instruments. A student group calling itself the "Kendall Band Preservation Society" was born. They work after-hours to jury-rig whatever fixes are necessary. While the repair schedule can be scattershot, the hammers continue to swing 30 years after their installation.

Yet whether the chimes are dormant or active, the sculptures hang, safely tucked between the third-rails heading in either direction. They are relics of an inspired attempt to bring music to a drab, workaday port of daily commutes.

# TAZA FACTORY TOUR

## 29

*True grit*

561 Windsor Street
Tuesday–Friday 11am–6pm, Saturday–Sunday 10am–6pm
Visit tazachocolate.com for latest tour information
Green Line/Union

n 2005, Alex Whitmore founded Taza after visiting Oaxaca, Mexico, and trying stoneground chocolate for the first time. The texture was rustic and gritty, the flavors bold and bright. The Oaxacan method for making chocolate let the nuances of the cacao beans come through in the finished product. A Hershey bar this was not.

The chocolate makers were using machinery that seemed simple – little rotary mills with rounded stones to grind up roasted beans. But, as Whitmore would learn, the mills contained secrets closely held by the *molineros*, or millers.

Each millstone is carved – or, in the craft, "dressed" – with specific patterns of grooves that produce just the right grind for finished products. Corn, cacao, chiles, wheat, rice: each requires its own carefully considered set of angled furrows and parallel channels, known to the molineros alone. Whitmore apprenticed with a molinero after much pleading and returned to Somerville determined to bring a new kind of chocolate to the States.

Visitors who tour the factory see first-hand how the full process works. Roasted cacao beans are converted into cacao nibs, then into a paste called "chocolate liquor," to which cane sugar is added to create something called "chocolate mass." After further refinement, the mass is poured into molds and becomes the finished Taza bars or discs.

While the visuals aren't exactly Willy Wonka – there are miles of pipes and large machines that resemble industrial washer-dryers – rarely-talked-about secrets of the chocolate trade are shared openly. Where big corporate producers roast their beans at 500 degrees Fahrenheit in order to create uniformity of taste (read: boringness), Taza roasts the beans for its bars at just 235 degrees Fahrenheit to heighten their flavor.

In one of the work rooms, every surface (and stapler) seems to be in need of housecleaning; they're actually covered in a fine chocolate dust that is a natural product of the de-shelling process. And every one of those pipes is encased in warm water to prevent the liquid chocolate within from solidifying. If it does, it will take five hours to restore flow.

To this day, those secret millstones are the key to the whole process. Whitmore still personally carves each by hand. About once a month, due to wear, the patterns are recarved into every stone, and after about seven years, the millstones are completely worn out.

# FLUFF FESTIVAL

*Marshmallow mayhem*

*Union Square, held yearly in late September*
*Visit flufffestival.com for the most current information*
*Green Line/Union*

"Fluff" is a condiment made and consumed almost exclusively in New England. The sticky spread is essentially viscous marshmallow, and it is most often used to make a sandwich called a "fluffernutter" – a sinfully indulgent riff on peanut butter and jelly: two slices of white bread, peanut butter on one, marshmallow fluff on the other. Put them together and enter sugary nirvana.

Fluff was invented in Somerville in 1917 by Archibald Query, who cooked it up at home and sold it door-to-door. The recipe has just four components: sugar syrup, corn syrup, dried egg whites, and vanilla flavoring.

When World War I caused sugar shortages, Query moved on from his foray in Fluff peddling. He later sold the recipe for $500 to two American soldiers returning home, H. Allen Durkee and Fred L. Mower. The new Durkee-Mower Company soon had local pantries well stuffed with Fluff (which, for a short time, they rebranded Toot Sweet Marshmallow Fluff.)

In the 1950s, Durkee-Mower moved manufacturing to nearby Lynn and, in 1961, their ad agency changed the sandwich game forever, pitching the company on the name "Fluffernutter." The term was quickly trademarked and has been owned by the company ever since. (And protected: Durkee-Mower sued William-Sonoma in 2006 for misuse of the name.)

Local pride in Fluff is intense. In 2014, a bill naming the Fluffernutter Massachusetts's official state sandwich passed the State House of Representatives.

Since 2006, Somerville has held a yearly "What the Fluff?" Festival to celebrate Fluff's legacy and bright future. Fluff-themed art, clothing, Christmas ornaments, and handmade knick-knacks are sold at stands decked out with the jar's iconic label. Culinary invention is everywhere, from Fluff donuts to Fluff-infused Mexican horchata, Fluff-dressed sweet potato fries to Fluff-filled pierogis. Men are encouraged to massage Fluff into their beards for unique styling.

A volunteer dressed as Archibald Query serves as master-of-ceremonies, and a group of scantily clad "Flufferettes" mingle and perform burlesque.

## The "Flufferettes"

The "Flufferettes" dancers are just the latest iteration of a long tradition in Fluff history: in 1930, Durkee-Mower began sponsoring a radio show featuring the "Flufferettes" singing upbeat jingles about marshmallow dreams.

# NEON WILLIAMS SHOP

*Preserving a kinetic glow*

*86 R Joy Street*
*neonwilliams.com*
*Email contact@neonwilliams.com or call 617 623 9370 to arrange a visit*
*The workshop is active during normal business hours*
*Green Line/Union Square*

Inside a nondescript industrial building, surrounded by chain-link fences and empty sidewalks, one of the last remaining neon sign shops in New England is practicing a near-forgotten art and preserving hundreds of vintage signs that would otherwise be destroyed.

Founded in 1934, Neon Williams has produced tens of thousands of signs for theaters, motels, restaurants, bars, museums, universities, and sporting arenas. While the company has gone by many names – most descriptively the W.M. Croft "Long Life Neon Tubes" Company – it has survived changing public tastes and the emergence of cheaper technologies.

In 2018, the shop was set to close. But one of its customers – Dave Waller, a neon sign collector – stepped in with his wife, Lynn, and a graphic designer friend to save the business. Dave is a fount of neon history and speaks poetically about its unique light quality, which he terms "kinetic." He also asserts that no other light source can be shaped to captivate people, to display such a wide array of colors, and to delight as both itself and whatever it's bent to represent.

While Dave has built a museum display in the lobby that explains neon technology, the real treasures are the hundreds of antique signs hanging from every surface of the shop. Huge displays of glowing food, beers, larger-than-life characters, and the names of long-lost bars and restaurants abound. A pornographic sign shows a woman bending over indelicately. An oversized cowboy lassoes a chicken.

Visitors will get to see some of the glass artists at work bending, a skill Dave reveres: "There's no way to do things like this without doing your 10,000 hours...and the only way to get your time in is to be in the fires and feel that glass and the way it's bending, and there's a moment where it's perfectly suitable to bend. And if it's too hot, it collapses and you wreck it. And if it's too cold, you don't get a good bend."

Neon Williams's work can be seen all over Boston: "If it's a big neon sign around here, we do the glasswork for it," notes Dave. Check out the Paramount Theatre, Union Square Oyster House, The Sinclair, and Cheapo Records in Cambridge. The firm also regularly creates neon art for Hollywood productions and, oddly, light sources for automakers to calibrate their paint color machines.

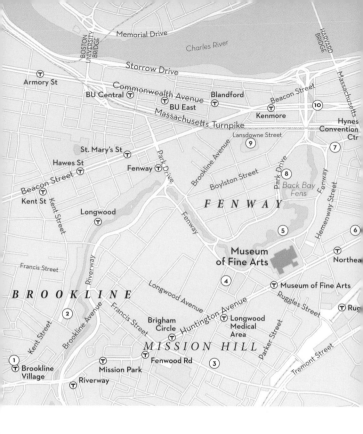

# Brookline, Fenway, Back Bay

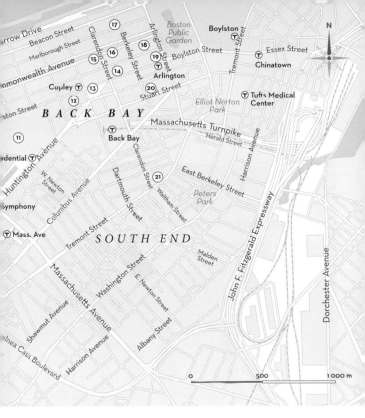

# PUPPET SHOWPLACE THEATER ①

## *Powerful puppets*

*32 Station Street*
*puppetshowplace.org*
*Library of puppet-related tomes: by appointment only*
*Green Line/Brookline Village*

Since its founding in June 1974, the Puppet Showplace Theater has been a cozy place to go and take in a show. The theater's whimsical front lobby is a portal to another world, with oversized puppet masks mounted on the wall and other seemingly homemade creations peeking out at visitors from odd angles. The theater itself, built in a former storefront, is a simple bricked-in box with room for under 100 audience members. There isn't a bad seat in the house.

The theater began as a passion project of Mary Churchill, an elementary school educator who used puppets to help children struggling to learn how to read. What began as a classroom tool soon blossomed into a proper theater troupe, the Cranberry Puppets. Churchill specialized in fairy tales performed by crocheted hand puppets.

Each year the Puppet Showplace Theater holds over 300 performances and workshops, covering all manner of puppetry – hand puppets, marionettes, shadow puppets, Punch-and-Judy style "booth shows," and Muppet-like mouth puppets. Look out for the much-anticipated yearly visits from the Tanglewood Marionettes, which tend to sell out quickly.

While many of the shows are aimed at children, the theater also hosts workshops for puppet-curious adults, ranging from "Cardboard Construction" to "Puppet Improv." A few times a year, the theater also hosts Puppet Slams, a nighttime venue for adult-focused shows, which can include comedic shorts, risqué and avant-garde material, and children's show in development. It's a rare occasion to see many types of puppetry back-to-back, performed by amateurs and professionals alike.

The theater keeps alive the memory of its founder through its Mary Churchill Memorial Fund, which covers the cost of tickets for low-income students to attend shows.

Further, Mary first learned about the art of puppetry through books, and the theater is home to a library of puppet-related tomes (how-tos, puppet histories), which can be browsed by appointment only.

# THE DUTCH HOUSE

*A former pavilion at the 1893 Chicago World's Fair*

*20 Netherlands Road*
*Green Line/Longwood*

Bedecked with ornamental sculpture and painted shutters, the four-story Dutch House began its life as a chocolate company's exhibition hall at the 1893 Chicago World's Fair.

The Van Houten Cocoa Company created the structure as a temporary pavilion for cocoa classes and tastings and to show off Dutch-inspired interiors. The house was designed by Dutch architect G. Weyman and manufactured in the Netherlands and Belgium, then taken apart, shipped to Illinois, and rebuilt at one end of the Manufactures and Liberal Arts Building, the largest building on earth at the time.

A contemporary account described the Dutch House as: "Being made of wood, outside it is only a poor imitation of a steep-roofed, ordinary Dutch brick house, but inside everything is certainly most picturesquely arranged...A wainscoting of Delft tiles harmonizes with blackened woodwork, and the windows throughout the building are of pale olive-green glass in leaded panes...The whole picturesque interior is increased by the costumes of serving-girls, who wear the curious coiffures of the different districts of Holland."

Competition was fierce for visitor attention; other chocolate makers constructed a full windmill, a 7.5 foot tall statue of Christopher Columbus made entirely of chocolate, and a temple built of 30,000 pounds of chocolate.

But the Dutch House captured the attention of fair attendee and Brookline resident Captain Charles Brooks Appleton, who purchased the whole of it at an auction when the World's Fair closed its doors. According to the 1925 minutes of the Brookline Historical Society, "the building was taken apart, brought to Brookline, and erected on Netherlands Road." (The report also notes Appleton was "much interested in the cavalry and was a member of many patriotic societies" and was "missed by us all.")

## A replica of a 1591 house in the Netherlands

The Dutch House is a replica of the 1591 City Hall in Franeker, Netherlands, with a front doorframe modeled on that of the Enkhuizen Orphanage. Modern restoration work has enlivened the doorframe with animals and mermaids based on the original sculpting. The house has passed through many hands and is today a private home.

# CRUTCH DISPLAY

*A collection of miracles*

*Our Lady of Perpetual Help Church*
*1545 Tremont Street*
*Monday–Friday 7am–1pm, Saturday 4pm–5pm, Sunday 9am–5pm*
*Orange Line/Roxbury Crossing*

In 1901, the Catholic Basilica and Shrine of Our Lady of Perpetual Hope was described as "A Lourdes in the Land of Puritans," reflecting the church's widespread reputation as a site of miraculous healing.

Stories abound of devout Catholics being cured of all kinds of ailments – cancer, blindness, deafness, lameness – after prayer to an image of Our Lady of Perpetual Hope.

Mounted in a chapel to the left of the main altar, a Byzantine-style Mary holds the baby Jesus while Archangels Michael and Gabriel hover above wielding the tools of the crucifixion. It is a copy of an original kept in Rome at the Church of Saint Alphonsus Maria de Liguori; that image, too, is credited with miraculous healing.

Each side of the Boston chapel is festooned with towering racks of crutches, braces, and canes that have been left behind by the cured. Many show signs of their age and use and clearly predate modern medical care.

The first miracle attributed to the Boston image occurred on 28 May 1871, the very first day it was publicly venerated. Louisa Julia Kohler, a young girl suffering from intense pain in her ankle, was completely healed, save for a scar. According to a history of the church entitled "The Glories of Mary in Boston," several days after her recovery, Louisa studied a small statue of Jesus dead on Mary's lap, and joyfully exclaimed, "Face like papa; foot like mine!" Indeed, the history asserts, "[a]s a matter of fact, the scar on the child's foot closely resembled the mark of the wound on Our Lord's."

But it was an 1883 case that made the shrine famous among believers and a place of pilgrimage. At the age of 4, Grace Hanley, the daughter of a Civil War veteran, was thrown from a carriage and broke her spine on a small rock. The injury caused continuous pain, headaches, and near paralysis of her legs. When Grace turned 12, following years of grisly medical treatments involving electrical shocks, icebags, and heavy leather corsets, her family performed a novena at the shrine, a Catholic tradition of nine days of prayer and contemplation. On the ninth day, during mass, Grace miraculously stood up, pain-free, and walked to the altar, then to her home and up a flight of stairs. Her ailments had entirely vanished.

Hanley's miracle is honored with a plaque at the chapel.

# STAINED GLASS FRAGMENTS

④

*Remains from Reims Cathedral in France saved by a U.S. ambulance driver*

*Isabella Stewart Gardner Museum*
*First floor*
*25 Evans Way*
*Saturday–Monday 10am–5pm, Thursday 11am–9pm, Friday 11am–5pm*
*Closed Tuesday*
*Green Line E/Museum of Fine Arts or Orange Line/Ruggles*

The Isabella Stewart Gardner Museum houses a vast private collection of art displayed in the collector's opulent mansion. Amid the Titians and Michelangelos, it can be easy to miss the less famous treasures. On the first floor of the house is an open gallery called the Chinese Loggia, named for its collection of Buddhist sculptures. Set in an otherwise transparent window, an easily overlooked work of oddly-shaped stained glass seems dissonant with the Asian-inspired surroundings.

These colorful shards are the remains of once famous stained glass windows from Reims Cathedral in France, which was bombed and set aflame in 1914 by the German military in World War I. Crews began to repair the Gothic masterpiece in 1919; it did not reopen to the public until 1938.

The broken pieces of stained glass were pocketed by an American ambulance driver named Chester Howell in 1918, four years after the initial bombing. Howell attested, "I obtained from among the ruins of the Cathedral there a hundred and five fragments of the glass windows, several groups of such pieces being still held together in their original leading…there seemed daily probability of the capture of Rheims, and small likelihood of the French being able to save even what little of value still remained in the city."

Gardner had them reconfigured in a modern design by her friend Henry Davis Sleeper, renowned interior designer and a member of "Dabsville" – a coterie of artists based in nearby Gloucester.

In the new setting, the glass remains create an enchanting mosaic of irregular shapes and bright colors. Visitors can still see the faces of – what? The Faithful? Saints? Prophets? Lepers? – etched into several jagged pieces.

That an ambulance driver is behind this magical piece is fitting: during the war, Gardner gave financial support to the American Field Service operation in France. Founded by yet another close friend of Gardener's named A. Piatt Andrew, the AFS provided ambulance service to French soldiers and civilians. In 1914, before the U.S. had entered the war, Andrew decamped to France and served as an ambulance driver. Gardner sponsored an ambulance dubbed "Y" after her nickname of "Ysabel."

# JAPANESE TEMPLE BELL

*Scrapped, saved, stolen*

*The Fens, enter by Forsyth Way*
*The bell is just across the footbridge*
*Green Line/Museum of Fine Arts or Orange Line/Ruggles*

A historical and cultural artifact with tales to tell, a massive 450-pound Japanese bell sits close to the border of The Fens park with very little to indicate its extraordinary history.

The bell was forged in 1675 and, for hundreds of years, rang out during Buddhist ceremonies at the Manpuku-ji Temple in the northern Japanese city of Sendai.

Due to the military demands of World War II, hundreds of these ancient temple bells – called *Bonshō* – were melted down by the Japanese government and reconstituted as artillery. It's estimated that 95% of Japan's original temple bells were lost in this way and, while re-creations have since been forged, Boston's is the last World War II bell still in the United States.

Shortly after Japan's surrender, this temple bell was rescued from a scrapheap in Yokosuka by the American Navy crew of the *USS Boston*. The sailors brought the bell back to San Francisco in 1946 and then shipped it to Boston for a whopping $42.80. Once it arrived in the Northeast, it was placed on display in Boston Common and later relocated to its current location.

A number of other bells similarly found their way to the States during the war, but they were eventually repatriated. In 1952, the State Department attempted to do the same with Boston's bell, but the people of Sendai insisted that the city keep it as a symbol of peace.

Care for the bell waned over the years. Though there is no record of who did it, the brass was painted black for a time, then later restored. In 2004, robbers attempted to steal the bell and it sustained some surface damage. It was last restored in 2011, and today appears in fine shape.

---

Note the bell handle's whimsical dragon design, which could have come straight out of modern anime. Interestingly, Bonshō do not have clappers, but are rung by striking the exterior of the bell with a wooden dowel.

---

In 1954, a Japanese organization called the World Peace Bell Association was founded with the goal of installing temple bells in every country around the world as symbols of peace. The United Nations in New York has a modern replica temple bell that is struck twice a year: on Earth Day and at the opening of the yearly UN General Assembly.

# NATIONAL BRAILLE PRESS TOUR ⑥

*Handbound books for the blind*

*88 St. Stephen Street*
*Tours need to be booked two weeks in advance*
*Arrange by calling 617-425-2416 or email contact@nbp.org*
*Orange Line or Purple Line/Ruggles*

Tucked into a townhouse on a quiet street, the National Braille Press at first feels more like an accounting office than the leading Braille publisher in the United States. But, as visitors will discover, below a few floors of sleepy offices (the press has been in this spot since 1946) sit the stars of the show: giant, heavy black metal Heidelberg printing machines, which look like holdovers from the Industrial Revolution. They resemble small-scale steam engines, right down to the gauges, unlabeled knobs and levers, and miscellaneous hand cranks.

The Heidelbergs churn out up to 20,000 pages of Braille per hour, an impressive – and necessary – speed, given that Braille books must be larger and more voluminous than standard books to accommodate the system's six dots per letter "cell." Throughout the tour, workers laughed uproariously recalling the size of their Braille-edition "Harry Potter" series, which required stacks and stacks.

Those stacks – along with thousands of other pages each year – are organized and bound by volunteers and a small, vigorous cadre of visually impaired workers.

The press is a nonprofit and built on the idea that blind people should be able to pay the same price for a book as sighted people do. The cost to produce a book in Braille is three times more expensive than the cost to produce a book meant to be read: the text has to be transcribed, then proofread and embossed onto zinc sheets, pressed into specialized paper, and finally hand assembled and stitched. Nonetheless, the National Braille Press sells its books for the same prices they would go for at an average bookstore. The press produces 5,000 books per year across about 100 titles, ranging from children's books to religious tracts. The titles show the insight the nonprofit has into the needs of the visually impaired: "We printed a 'One Pot Cooking' cookbook because, when you're blind, you can't be dealing with two pots." Braille Red Sox game schedules lie about the office here and there.

The press also ships to readers around the world, where Braille books can be hard to find. A post office cart was filled with packages labeled "Nigeria," "Bangladesh," and "Kenya."

# MASSACHUSETTS HISTORICAL SOCIETY

## *Grab bag of American history*

*1154 Boylston Street*
*Monday, Wednesday and Friday 10am–4:45pm, Tuesday 10am–7:45pm,*
*Saturday 10am–3pm*
*Green Line/Hynes Convention Center*

**F**ounded in 1791 by 10 history lovers led by the Reverend Jeremy Belknap, the Massachusetts Historical Society is the oldest such organization in the U.S. Its collection of 12 million items spans American history and preserves extraordinary – and extraordinarily odd – artifacts, documents, art, and bric-a-brac.

The society is housed in a three-story brick building constructed in 1899. It features galleries and library rooms that are open to the public. The society emphasizes rotating exhibits and maintains no permanent display, so visitors should be ready for surprises – coming upon, perhaps, the pen Abraham Lincoln used to sign the Emancipation Proclamation, George Washington's epaulets from the 1781 Siege of Yorktown, or the copper weathervane of a scantily clad Native American archer that topped the Province House of Massachusetts's colonial governors. (see p. 54)

While the society's collections are rich with important historical documents – including the personal papers of Presidents John Adams, Thomas Jefferson, and John Quincy Adams – no artifact is too obscure for the organization's curation. An imposing black paperweight of a hot dog was given to vice-presidential candidate Henry Cabot Lodge Jr. by the National Hot Dog Council in 1960, with a note reading: "A million miles of hot dogs will be consumed in the United States this year and we hope that every one of the hot dog lovers casts a vote for you and Dick Nixon." (They didn't.)

Some pieces tie directly to the state's history, including a bottle filled with tea leaves collected on Dorchester Neck the day after the Boston Tea Party in 1773. An oak chest of drawers from the 17th century is known as the "Witch Bureau" because of its supposed role as evidence in the Salem Witch Trials (the estate that donated the furniture reported that "from the middle drawer…one of the Witches jumped out who was hung on Gallows Hill, in Salem.") The MHS also holds the papers of the Witch Trial Judge Samuel Sewall and a piece of wood from a tree used for hanging guilty witches.

A recent visit highlight was the MHS's Warner Spoon Collection – a trove of souvenir utensils gathered by a globe-trotting couple in the 1800s. An ornate silver spoon features a fantastical scene of a cherub reading a book surrounded by angels, birds, fish, flowers, and a satyr.

# FENWAY VICTORY GARDENS

*WWII relics bloom anew each spring*

*1200 Bolyston Street, within the The Fens*
*Open dawn to dusk all year, but best visited June – September*
*Green Line/Hynes Convention Center*

Following the attack on Pearl Harbor in December 1941, the United States found itself on a war footing. Diverting national resources to support the growing military effort, the U.S. government instituted rationing and called on average citizens to plant so-called "Victory Gardens" – vegetable patches that would relieve stress on food production and cost. Promotional posters claimed "Our food is fighting" and "Your country needs soybeans for Food, Feed, Guns." The movement was startlingly successful: an estimated two-thirds of American households took to the garden; First Lady Eleanor Roosevelt oversaw a harvest of beans, cabbage, carrots, and tomatoes on the White House lawn (over the objections of FDR.)

In 1942, the City of Boston opened public parkland to citizens in the form of community plots on The Fens, one of landscape architect Frederick Law Olmsted's iconic Emerald Necklace parks.

While the defeat of Germany and Japan in 1945 saw the dissipation of the gardening trend, these 500 Fenway Victory Gardens still occupy 7.5 lush acres and are kept up by 375 local community volunteers. The Fenway Victory Gardens are one of only two continuously run World War II gardens in existence – and the only one still operating on the same footprint.

Today, the process of landing one of the garden patches is competitive and would-be gardeners have to join a waitlist and abide by a strict set of rules and regulations to remain "in good standing." However, it would be hard to argue it's not worth it to own a little patch of bucolic wonder smack in the middle of bustling Boston.

One of the joys of visiting the gardens is observing the variety of designs and types of gardens the members tend. They range from leisure gardens – complete with stone paths, garden furniture, and tchotchke decorations – to fruit, herb, and vegetable patches to perennial and shade gardens. On a warm summer day, friends and family lounge amid their greenery, soaking in the sun.

There are public areas to sit and relax, but wandering the somewhat overgrown paths between patches is the true draw. Don't miss the unique ADA-accessible garden, which meets requirements of the Americans with Disabilities Act by incorporating raised planting beds and wheelchair-accessible pathways.

# RED SEAT AT FENWAY PARK

*Watch your head*

*4 Yawkey Way*
*Visit mlb.com/redsox/ballpark/tours for tour times and tickets*
*Green Line/Kenmore*

Fenway Park, home of Boston's beloved Red Sox, is known as one of the quirkier national ballparks, not least for its oddly shaped 9 acre lot and 37 foot wall affectionately known as "The Green Monster."

Indeed, green dominates the stands across Fenway's 37,755 seats. But there is one that stands alone against this monocolor sea: Section 42, Row 37, Seat 21, which is painted a distinct strawberry red.

The seat honors the longest home run ever hit in the park. On 9 June 1946, baseball legend Ted Williams hit the ball 502 feet off a pitch by Fred Hutchinson of the Detroit Tigers.

At that game, a construction worker from Albany named Joseph A. Boucher, dressed up with a straw boater to shield him from the summer

sun, was perched in the stands. Williams's ball sped toward Boucher and hit him square on top of the head, piercing a hole straight through his hat. "BULLSEYE!" The *Boston Daily Globe* declared the next day.

Boucher was less than amused. As the *Globe* recounted it: "'How far away must one sit to be safe in this park?' asked Ted's target for the day, feeling his pate tenderly." Boucher also noted he didn't get to keep the ball, which bounced further into the stands.

While Boucher received first aid, he did not sustain any serious injury. The *Globe*'s Harold Kaese couldn't resist some colorful commentary on the hat, "in the crown of which was a soft label that acted as a cushion… It made a tidy little hole that speaks well for the quality of the headpiece. One of my straw hats, for instance, would have broken up like a mat of shredded wheat struck by a hammer."

While history is clear on Boucher's plight, it is not exactly the case that he was installed in the famed seat at the time. In 1946, Boucher and his compatriots would have been in open, unshaded bleachers. The park added seat backs in 1977, and Red Sox owner Haywood Sullivan installed the red seat as a memorial to the home run in 1984.

While the home run record stands, it has not been without controversy. In 2015, Red Sox slugger David Ortiz cast doubt that anyone could hit the ball that distance. But the team's own baseball analysts have run the numbers and concluded that Williams's accomplishment wasn't impossible; it just required a rare combination of strength, a steep launch angle off the bat, and favorable wind (which on the day was estimated at a significant 18 to 24 miles per hour).

It's also rather hard to argue with the picture of Boucher after the incident, his fingers thrusting through the hole in his damaged hat.

If you want to spot the red seat, arrive at a game early. Serious fans request it specifically and take pride in playing Boucher for a day.

## Initials in Morse code

Installed in 1934, the manual wooden scoreboard at the bottom of the Green Monster is still used today. Its 127 slots are updated with numbered cards by hand, despite Fenway's many digital displays. On the thin white stripe separating American League scores, note the series of dots and dashes: these represent, in Morse code, the initials of former owners Tom and Jean Yawkey, who owned the team from 1933 to 1992.

# STATUE OF A VIKING

*When a Harvard chemist reformulates history*

*Commonwealth Avenue near the Charlesgate overpass*
*Green Line/Hynes Convention Center*

The statues on the Commonwealth Avenue Mall are a who's-who of Massachusetts history: generals, abolitionists, statesmen…and a Viking warrior surveying nearby apartment buildings. Erected in 1887, the statue of Leif Erikson was donated to the city by Harvard Professor Eben Norton Horsford, who established the first modern chemistry

lab in the U.S. Horsford made a fortune by patenting baking powder and used his wealth to search for archeological evidence substantiating his belief that Erikson and a crew of Norsemen founded a settlement known as Norumbega on the banks of the Charles River. Modern archeologists remain steadfast that there is no truth to the theory.

This connection to a proud ancient culture – and a Protestant Norway – was a convenient fiction embraced by many of the elite "Boston Brahmin" set, who looked with anxiety at the growing numbers of Italian and Irish Catholic immigrants flooding Boston.

Crediting the discovery of America to Erikson meant that Columbus – that most celebrated Catholic – had no legitimate claim to fame.

The statue's base declares "Leif the Lucky Son of Erik" in runes, the Viking alphabet, and the dragon-headed prow of a ship juts out beneath.

Reliefs show a Viking hall bedecked in shields and weaponry and Norwegians scrambling up a rocky New England shore at the end of their long journey.

At the back of Erikson's head, amid flowing curls, sits a tiny, easily overlooked spiked cap, more yarmulke than helmet. The statue is based on a picture from a poetry collection, and that imagined Viking had a pointed hat, but bigger than the final statue's. It was all purely imagined.

Leif used to gaze out on the Charles River, but modern construction has boxed him in, securing his fate as Boston's most strapping Peeping Tom.

## Other vestiges of a made-up Nordic past

Buildings throughout the city feature the prows of Viking ships as carved stone ornaments. Good examples can be found near the roof of the Weld Boathouse in Cambridge at the juncture of Memorial Drive and Kennedy Street, and at the base of the flagpoles of the World Trade Center at 200 Seaport Boulevard in Boston.

Horsford didn't stop at the statue: he later claimed to have found archeological remains of Erikson's house in Cambridge – conveniently not far from Horsford's own – and commissioned a plaque reading: "On this spot in the year 100 Leif Erikson built his house in Vineland." You can still find the plaque on the grounds of Mount Auburn Hospital at the intersection of Mount Auburn Street and Gerry's Landing Road.

# RELIQUARY OF
# SAINT MAXIMILIAN KOLBE

*Holy beard hair in a replica of the Gates of Auschwitz*

*Saint Francis Chapel*
*800 Boylston Street*
*7:30am–5:30pm all days of the week*
*Green Line/Hynes Convention Center*

The Prudential Center, Boston's second tallest building, is crammed with offices, but at street level it is a high-end mall. Hidden past the bougie yoga pants shops, just around the corner from a bevy of fast food spots, is a surprise: a humble Catholic chapel. The Saint Francis Chapel is a peaceful space for shoppers to squeeze in a rosary or mass, even amid the capitalist free-for-all outside its doors.

While the chapel itself looks unremarkable, it contains a fascinating artifact of World War II. To the right of the altar, three reliquaries are on display. Reliquaries are containers for relics – objects of religious significance related to the life of Jesus or saints. Relics are often body parts – bone, hair, a limb. They are meant to be venerated, not worshipped, an act reserved for God. Often, reliquary designs relate to the relic within.

The reliquary of Saint Maximilian Kolbe may look disturbingly familiar. It features an oddly curved sign between two poles – a replica of the Gates of Auschwitz, the infamous Nazi concentration camp. Where Auschwitz's sign read, "ARBEIT MACHT FREI" – German for "WORK WILL SET YOU FREE" – the reliquary's message is Latin and translates to "THE TRUTH WILL SET YOU FREE," a biblical quote from Jesus.

Kolbe was a Polish friar renowned for antagonizing the Nazis. He was arrested in February 1941 and sent to Auschwitz. At the camp, he gave his life to save that of fellow prisoner Franciszek Gajowniczek, a Polish Army sergeant who was sentenced to death as retaliation for a prisoner escape. Kolbe asked to be killed instead and was injected with carbonic acid; Gajowniczek survived the war and died in 1995. For his selfless act, Kolbe was canonized as a martyr and saint by Pope John Paul II in 1982.

The relic itself, which is viewable, is the saint's beard hair, preserved in the shape of a cross. The hair was saved by a fellow friar after Kolbe shaved off his long beard. The brother sensed that Kolbe's passion and devotion may well result in sainthood.

## The vision of Saint Maximilian

The poles of the reliquary are topped by two crowns, which relate to a vision of Saint Maximilian's. When he was a boy, the Virgin Mary appeared to him and presented two crowns – one white for purity and one red for martyrdom. She asked which he would like, and the boy responded he would accept them both.

# THE GOOSE GIRL CERAMIC

*Saturday Evening Girls and Paul Revere Pottery*

*700 Boylston Street*
*Monday–Thursday 9am–8pm, Friday–Saturday 9am–5pm, Sunday 11am–5pm*
*Green Line/Copley*

On a wall of the Children's Room in the Boston Public Library there is a beautiful ceramic tile art piece that looks both hand-made and handsome: The Goose Girl.

It is the work of the "Saturday Evening Girls," a club of young women, mostly poor Italian or Jewish immigrants who resided in Boston's North End at the turn of the 20th century. The club was the invention of philanthropist Helen Storrow (wife of investment banker James J. Storrow, for whom Boston's major thoroughfare Storrow Drive is named) and an enterprising librarian named Edith Guerrier.

This was the Progressive Era, with social and political reforms aplenty, all seeking to level the playing field, democratize education and opportunity, and improve conditions for the poor or disenfranchised. However, many of these reforms were aimed at helping disadvantaged men.

Guerrier and Storrow saw a need, and they filled it. The Saturday Evening Girls began as a book club that met on Saturday nights, targeted specifically at girls living in the overcrowded North End ghettos. The meetings were meant to expand on the girls' basic public education, to give them access to notable Boston intellectuals through lectures and discussion, and to provide exposure to music and the arts.

Guerrier was inspired to start similar clubs for girls of different ages on other nights of the week. (Think "Friday Evening Girls," etc.)

In 1906, Storrow paid for Guerrier and her partner to tour Europe, and they returned with a business idea for the SEG: a pottery studio emulating the folk art of poor ceramics makers across the ocean. Soon, the Saturday Evening Girls founded Paul Revere Pottery, based in an apartment close to Revere's famed Old North Church. The shop gave the Saturday Evening Girls a way to make money in a safe, even pleasant, working environment; while some women worked, others read literature aloud to the group.

Paul Revere Pottery stayed in operation through 1942. Its works trumpet their proudly handcrafted style and often feature flat matte-colors with bold black lines and white spaces to create natural settings or whimsical animals. Several Saturday Evening Girls – most notably Sara Galner – developed quite an advanced technique, examples of which are held by the Museum of Fine Arts in Boston and the Met Museum in New York.

# 16TH CENTURY VENETIAN PRINTER DEVICES

*Nearly forgotten marks*

*700 Boylston Street*
*Green Line/Copley*

The main Boston Public Library building is awash in symbolic words and art – the names of great Massachusetts citizens, lions, allegorical figures, statues of political figures. Most are staid and traditional.

But along the exterior of the building, high above street level, placed between the upper window arches, are 33 granite medallions that perplex attentive passersby.

They are beautiful, but the imagery doesn't seem to fit a Great American Library. Some highlights:

A disembodied hand emerging from clouds to grasp an anchor.

An infant holding a torch, surrounded by winged serpents.

A three-headed person – with the heads of an old man, a woman, and a young man.

A crab seeming to attack – or maybe hug? – a butterfly.

The motley collection is the work of Spanish sculptor Domingo Mora, circa 1895. Thirty-one of the medallions represent the devices or colophons – essentially, the logos – of early booksellers and printers, mostly Venetian and from the 16th century. (The other two represent a modern U.S. printer and a medal honoring the invention of the printing press.) The medallions were originally conceived as a set of 50, with the seals of great universities in the U.S. and Europe.

Mora devoted himself to discovering these obscure marks in original works. He then enlarged and sculpted their likenesses, thus saving them from obscurity. According to the 1899 *Handbook of the New Library in Boston*, the marks were "often woodcuts of the rudest description," making Mora's handiwork all the more extraordinary.

The oddity of the imagery, though, is attributed to Mora's method of selection: "The marks were chosen, it should be remembered, not so much for the reputation of the printer as for their decorative effect, and, as a result, a number of comparatively obscure men were included." Indeed, one odd medallion remains unidentified: four children's heads, mouths puckered as they blow mighty winds.

Look also for a dolphin wrapped around an anchor – this is the device of Aldus Manutius, who founded a press house in Venice in 1494 and went on to accrue a series of firsts: he was the first to print works by Aristotle and Sophocles, the first to use italics, the first to define how semicolons and commas should be used on the page, and the first to print small portable books like today's paperbacks.

# SAVED NATURAL HISTORY DIORAMAS

*Tiny histories*

*New England Life Insurance Building*
*501 Boylston Street*
*Lobby is accessible during normal business hours*
*Orange Line/Back Bay*

The impressive building at 234 Berkeley used to be home to the New England Museum of Natural History, from its construction in 1863 to the institution's rebranding as the Museum of Science in 1951 (when it moved to its current location.) Black-and-white photos show a big space full of glass cases and suspended skeletons, a classic cabinet-of-curiosities vibe. It is one of the city's lost treasures; today the building is a high-dollar home goods showroom.

By good fortune, four dioramas commissioned for the original museum by the Boston Society of Natural History are preserved in a corporate lobby just down the block. The art deco New England Life Insurance Building at 501 Boylston was constructed beginning in 1939, taking the place of two buildings from MIT's original Boston campus.

The history dioramas are in the lobby near the Newbury Street entrance. Artist Sarah Ann Rockwell painstakingly crafted the scenes, with painted backdrops by Henry Brooks. The attention to detail is astounding. The scenes cover Boston history from 2500 BC to 1863.

In the first diorama, Native Americans construct a fishweir – a complicated fence-like fish trap – just like that discovered under Boylston Street by subway workers in 1913.

The second diorama focuses on Reverend William Blaxton, who came to America from England in 1623 and is considered Boston's first settler. He is shown establishing a home on the Shawmut Peninsula.

The third shows the filling in of Boston's Back Bay by workers in 1858. It took two and a half decades to complete the landfill project (much of the land was transported from Needham, 25 miles from Back Bay) and the current neighborhood's watery name commemorates this legacy.

And the fourth diorama, ironically, depicts the former home of the dioramas: the old Natural History Museum. Next door, construction is just beginning on MIT's Rogers Hall.

### *"The place of his seclusion became the seat of a great city."*

When the Puritans arrived in 1630, William Blaxton, who disagreed with their harsh approach to Christianity, sold them his homestead of 50 acres – which would later become Boston Common; Blaxton then relocated to Rhode Island. Blaxton's place in the city's history is acknowledged on two plaques on Beacon Street, just across from the Common. One notes "The place of his seclusion became the seat of a great city."

# FIRST BAPTIST CHURCH TOWER FRIEZES

*Abraham Lincoln on a church tower*

*First Baptist Church*
*110 Commonwealth Avenue*
*Orange Line/Back Bay*

The First Baptist Church, also known as the Brattle Square Church, has been in the heart of Back Bay since 1882. However, the origins of its congregation stretch back to 1665, a time when Puritan leaders called heresy on the Baptists for arguing against the baptism of infants. The Baptists went underground, worshipped in private homes, then headed to Noddle's Island in the harbor where they would meet in a sanctuary masquerading as a tavern.

The church is easy to spot due to its enormous 176 foot square stone tower. The tower is unlike the more traditional steeples of Boston, which lean toward the Gothic; First Baptist's is low-peaked and Romanesque, with rounded arches and windows. (It is built largely of local Roxbury Puddingstone, see p. 208.)

© Daderot, CC0, via Wikimedia Commons

The tower's architect Henry Hobson Richardson later went on to build his masterpiece, Trinity Church on Copley Square, just a few blocks away.

The tower is striking not just for its height and style, but for an extraordinary set of friezes sculpted by Frederic Auguste Bartholdi, the Frenchman best known for designing the Statue of Liberty. The sculpture was done by Italian artisans *in situ* from plaster mock-ups designed by Bartholdi himself.

Bartholdi could not have anticipated the far-reaching effects of some of his artistic choices. Each corner is graced by an angel bearing a long straight horn; these were originally painted gold and, paired with Boston's long association with a certain set of legumes, led to an unfortunate nickname for First Baptist – "The Church of the Holy Bean-Blowers."

The scenes themselves are based on the Holy Sacraments, or, as Bartholdi would have it, "The Four Stages of the Christian Life." The sides represent Baptism, Communion, Marriage, and Death. Bartholdi cheekily slipped famous faces into each of the scenes.

On Baptism, Senator and abolitionist (and man famously caned by an opponent on the Senate chamber floor) Charles Sumner appears. Communion features writers Ralph Waldo Emerson, Nathaniel Hawthorne, and Henry Wadsworth Longfellow. Marriage got Italian General Giuseppe Garibaldi and, sitting contemplatively (or perhaps bored) with chin resting upon his hand, President Abraham Lincoln.

Bartholdi seems to have also inserted himself into the sculpture – perhaps on all four sides – though that is still debated among historians.

© Adrian Scottow, via Wikimedia Commons

# SRILA PRABHUPADA STATUE

*A boat to enlightenment*

*72 Commonwealth Avenue*
*Green Line/Arlington*

SEPTEMBER 17, 1965

A.C. BHAKTIVEDANTA
SWAMI PRABHUPADA

ARRIVED BY CARGO SHIP FROM INDIA
TO SHARE LORD KRISHNA'S
PHILOSOPHY AND CULTURE
WITH THE WORLD

*Somehow or other, O Lord, you have brought me here
to speak about you. Now, my Lord, it is up to you
to make me a success or failure as you like.*

On one of Boston's toniest streets, amid high-priced cars and fancy dogs, there stands a curious statue: a small bald man, in a robe, with a suitcase in hand and an umbrella under one arm. A long set of stairs disappears behind him, right into the side of half of an enormous steamship.

The building behind the statue is indistinguishable from the brick mansions that surround it but holds a secret: this is the Boston home of the International Society for Krishna Consciousness, known to most as Hare Krishna. The man is Srila Prabhupada, founder of the movement, and the statue depicts his arrival in the United States. While New York City is recognized as the launching point for the Hare Krishna movement (it kicked off with a chant in Tompkins Square Park in 1966), Prabhupada actually first set foot in Boston, on Commonwealth Pier, on 17 September 1965.

At 69 years old, Prabhupada left Kolkata aboard a cargo ship called "Jaladuta," headed for the United States. Prabhupada had spent years translating Hindu philosophy into English, and now was the time to take the text on the road. On board, he suffered intense seasickness and two heart attacks, then a dream of the deity Krishna cured him. He stepped off the ship virtually unknown in America and went on to convert thousands and establish 108 temples before his death in 1977.

## The secret in the secret

The Boston statue also has a deeper secret: it is but one half of a full work. The other half depicts the left side of the ship, with Prabhupada ascending the stairs. He is ready to head to sea, come what may (and carrying the same suitcase and umbrella). United only once, the two halves together portray a harrowing tale of survival and faith. Fittingly, the embarkation scene is installed halfway around the world, at an ISKCON site in Kolkata.

While the date is flexible, one weekend each summer, adherents to the Hare Krishna movement celebrate the Ratha Yatra, or Festival of Chariots, right in the heart of Boston on Boylston Street. This usually buttoned-up New England town is transformed into a sea of bright saris and colorful flower garlands, banners, and flags. Songs and chants echo off the Boston Public Library. At the center of the festivity is a wagon loaded with even more flowers, several deities, and a life-sized likeness of Prabhupada.

# THE FRENCH LIBRARY

*Library with a wine cellar*

*53 Marlborough Street*
*Visit frenchlibrary.org for hours and upcoming events*
*Green Line/Arlington*

In upscale Back Bay, a beautifully renovated mansion dating back 1867 is home to the largest private collection of French books an periodicals in the U.S.

This is the French Library, a nonprofit dedicated to French language nd culture. The building contains 30,000 volumes, ranging from Babar o modern bestsellers, and hosts cultural events including concerts, film creenings, and lectures.

The library traces its roots to the Nazi occupation of France, which ade rallying support for French culture an existential concern. In July 940, U.S. supporters founded an organization called France Forever; s Boston chapter opened a modest collection of 500 French books onated by the local consulate. A plaque in today's Founders' Room onors the five American and five French founders.

From the late-40s to 1978, Edna Allen Doriot, the Bostonian wife f a French general, drove the library to professionalize. Edna even per- aaded artist Katharine Lane Weems to donate her home to the organi- ttion in 1961-62. (You can see the Doriots in a painting in the reading om on the second floor.)

The library used the pause of in-person events during the COV- ) pandemic to renovate its reading rooms, which are now sun-filled nd beautifully appointed with modern furniture. The library is home o what must be the most chic children's room in history, complete ith fireplace and enormous gilded mirror. A dim back bedroom was ansformed into a home for discussion groups with what the library escribes as a "'chateau-style' chandelier and Queen of Spain wallpaper."

The nonprofit's leadership also made the startingly French decision › add a wine cellar, which now supports a range of gastronomic edu- ttion programs. The director of the library noted, "Wine is, of course, rance's national beverage, as well as a major export…[I]n collaboration ith the best local sommeliers, the French Library offers classes that rach how different wines pair with regional cuisine and local cheeses. he Library finds, as well, that its adult students appreciate the oppor- unity to learn about wines to become more conversant in the culture."

The organization hosts a rollicking Bastille Day Celebration every ıly 14. (A recent appetizer menu speaks to the authenticity of the or- ınization: "Croque-monsieur, Pissaladière, Saumon Fumé, Pâté de ımpagne/moutarde, Brie aux truffes, Cannelés.") Each December, its 1arché de Noël recreates the holiday markets of France.

When you visit, try to arrive close to the hour: the grandfather clock that chimes through the book-filled rooms was once that of Mildred Bixby, a library founder, lawyer, and pioneer for women's rights.

# PUPPET LENDING LIBRARY

*Marionettes need not apply*

*Newbury Street but is accessed via Public Alley 437 between Arlington and Berkeley Streets*
*Stop-in hours are 2–7pm on Tuesdays or call 617 378 5715 for an appointment*
*Orange Line/Back Bay*

Sara Peattie isn't just the keeper of the puppets; she is their creator. Peattie oversees the Puppet Lending Library, an eclectic collection of enormous, colorful puppets of her own design.

People come to Peattie to liven up their parades, pageants, school plays – any place they might need an enormous giraffe, a sinister 9 foot babushka, or a vaguely flirty sea creature.

"Some people just take one out for a walk around the Common," Peattie explains, wryly. "It's an experience!"

So is stepping into Peattie's workshop and puppet storage closet. Even the weirdly small door seems to indicate something special is behind it – a portal to Narnia, say, or at least a gnome's house. Every corner is packed with tools, brightly colored fabric, streamers, foam, papier mâché, cardboard, cellophane, and tangled bits of wire. Half-made or recently returned puppets recline at odd angles. A smiling elephant head was tossed crooked on the floor. An upsetting pig head rested on a shelf, its black eyes seeming to look into an unwelcome future. A bunch of ghoulish nuns might have been huddling for warmth.

It's a slightly nightmarish wonderland at every turn.

The library proper features rows and rows of standing puppets, roughly grouped by theme. Peattie's organization is vague: "This is the dragon section. Down there is the bird section. Down there is the fish section. This is the sarcastic blue people section."

Peattie is a luminary in the puppet world. She co-founded a nonprofit called the Puppeteers' Collective and has a partner puppet lending library in New York. She co-authored a book entitled "68 Ways to Make Really Big Puppets," with ideas ranging from "Wire Demon" to "Shimmy Dancer."

Asked if there are any marionettes in the collection, Peattie's eyes widen with indignation. "No! I have some simple two-string marionettes and even those I tangle up! You put them down carelessly and it's days and days!"

On nice days, Peattie heads out to the Boston Public Garden to give impromptu street performances.

# TIFFANY WINDOWS

*Fragile treasures*

*351 Boylston Street*
*Visit ascboston.org for tours and open hours*
*Green Line/Arlington*

1810    1889

In 1898, the Arlington Street Church approached Louis Tiffany, the son of jeweler Charles Tiffany, to create a set of 20 stained glass windows. While the manufacture of the windows stretched from 1899 to 1929, the designs were locked from the start, which gives the church the distinction of having the largest collection of Tiffany windows united by a single theme.

Louis Tiffany was an innovator in interior design following an early career in oil painting. He brought painterly attention to the details of his firm's windows and obsessed over technical execution. Early in his stint as a stained glass maker, Tiffany toured Europe to study the records of medieval artisans whose windows lived on in historic cathedrals across the continent.

Tiffany revived and invented forms of glass production that others considered too time-consuming or complicated. Where others would liberally paint details onto glass, Tiffany hated to block any light and stuck to painting only body parts.

Where other details were needed, Tiffany's artisans manipulated glass to achieve them. For example, look closely at the folds in the clothing worn by the windows' angels and saints: rather than simply apply paint to a flat pane, Tiffany and his workers physically folded and rippled molten glass in order to mimic flowing fabric.

Look at the trees and landscapes and you'll spy another Tiffany technique called "confetti glass." Tiffany would break very thin pieces of glass of various colors onto an iron table, then pour an additional layer of glass atop the shards to embed them in a single pane. The effect is like confetti preserved in amber, lending depth and randomness to the otherwise meticulously structured images.

Tiffany windows seem to have an inner light. The effect is achieved through the layering of glass of different colors – sometimes as many as six or seven deep. Look at the window showing an angel telling shepherds of Jesus's birth: below the angel's arm is the Star of Bethlehem, shining several layers down and apparently through the angel's garment.

While the plan called for 20 windows, funds dried up after the installation of number 16 and the onset of the Great Depression. Tiffany died in 1933; his studio went under. Thus, four windows remain jarringly empty, leaving the 16 Tiffany masterpieces to shine all the brighter.

*Steeped in history*

*330 Stuart Street*
*Orange Line/Back Bay*

Along an otherwise generic city block of corporate office entrances, there stands a historical and artistic shock: two enormous 12 foot bronze doors and an ornate doorframe carved with ancient religious symbols and a bevy of distinctly non-local animals: elephants.

The Salada Tea Company was founded in 1892 in Toronto but, in 1917, moved to an impressive new office and processing/packing facility in central Boston. The offices were decorated with Asian art – think Chinese lions and Oriental rugs – and the production facility was cutting-edge, with enormous leaf-cutting, dust-sifting, and tea-blending machines. The grand doors were commissioned by Salada's founder Peter Larkin, who revolutionized the trade by selling packaged tea in foil rather than offering loose leaves. The doors were installed in 1927 and, in the same year, won a prestigious silver medal at the Paris Salon in recognition of their beauty and craftsmanship.

The nearly 2-ton doors were produced by the Providence-based Gorham Company. Intricate bas-reliefs were sculpted by British artist Henry Wilson and, over 10 panels, bring to life the history, farming techniques, and transportation of Ceylon tea – a black tea cultivated in present-day Sri Lanka.

The upper panels show muscular men harvesting tea leaves and sorting them at tables. The lower panels show the men carrying loaded boxes of leaves on their heads, elephants laboring under even larger boxes, and, finally, ships taking on their caffeinated cargo. The space in between panels is richly decorated with patterns of tea leaves and tea berries.

The marble doorframe, designed by Wilson's assistant Caesar Caira, is impressive in its own right. A frieze of tromping elephants sits just below a sculpture of Demeter, the Greek goddess of the harvest. Persephone and Triptolemus, both Greek mythological figures associated with agriculture, round out the cross-cultural extravaganza.

The Salada Company manufactured from this building for over 40 years. While the site has changed hands many times since Salada vacated, the story of tea remains.

The name "Salada" itself comes from an ancient tea garden in Sri Lanka.

# THE CYCLORAMA AT THE BOSTON CENTER FOR THE ARTS

*History in the round*

*539 Tremont Street*
*Visit bostonarts.org/venue/the-cyclorama for upcoming events*
*Orange Line/Back Bay*

The Cyclorama is an enormous, breathtaking space: 127 feet across with a soaring copper dome that, when it was constructed in 1884, was the second largest dome in America.

While today the circular room is used for a mix of theater performances, trade shows, and private events, it was originally constructed to house a single enormous painting.

Popular in the U.S. and Europe, cycloramas were the virtual reality of the late 19th century: viewers stood on an elevated platform, often in the very center of the room, in order to lose themselves in a detailed, all-encompassing 360-degree scene. The effect was enhanced by real-life props – dirt, trees, rocks, weapons, costumed dummies – that stood in front of the giant mural.

The oil-on-canvas paintings invited guests to linger, searching out details and famous figures. The subjects of cyclorama paintings tended

Courtesy of Boston Center for the Arts; Photo by Melissa Blackall

toward the epic: grand battles, religious scenes, and tragedies. The Boston Cyclorama housed "The Battle of Gettysburg" by a French artist named Paul Philippoteaux, who spent weeks exploring the battlefield and speaking to Civil War veterans. While most Cyclorama paintings were lost, amazingly Philippoteaux's Boston work survives: clocking in at 377 feet long by 42 feet high and a whopping 12.5 tons, the painting hangs today at the National Park Service's Gettysburg National Military Park Museum in Pennsylvania.

The Boston Cyclorama was a popular attraction for about a decade, with well-attended hourly lectures explaining the historical context of the work. Then the crowds began to thin. "The Battle of Gettysburg" was crated up in a wooden box and, for years, stored outdoors.

While the building itself – originally a castle-like construction by Cummings and Sears, the same firm behind Boston's landmark Isabella Stewart Gardner Museum – underwent significant architectural changes, the great circular space within was preserved. Tenants came and went – the room was a boxing ring, a horse-riding facility, an auto shop, a sparkplug development facility. From 1923 to 1970, it was the HQ of a wholesale flower market.

In 1971, the Boston Center for the Arts took over the space and, once again, the Cyclorama became home to entertainment and educational programs throughout the year.

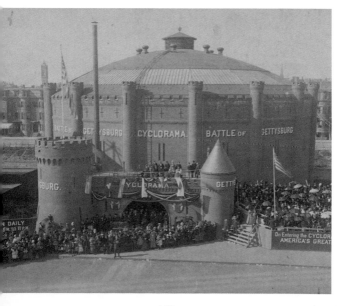

# West

# "NEIGHBORS" SCULPTURAL INSTALLATION

*A quiet neighborhood*

Forest Hills Cemetery
95 Forest Hills Avenue
The houses are extremely well hidden. Pick up a map of the cemetery and locate
White Oak Avenue. As you turn onto White Oak, there is a rock wall to your
right; the houses are nestled among the plants
Visit foresthillscemetery.com for open hours
Orange Line/Forest Hills

The graves of Forest Hills Cemetery are unpredictable. Some are grand temples to the interred, replete with sculpture and symbolism. Others are simple, even spare – just a name and two dates. The sheer size and variety of the cemetery's grounds and tombs can make a visitor dizzy, both directionally and philosophically. The rich and the poor, the artist and the patron, the plumber and the patriarch – all end up dwelling in the same place after death.

In 2006, sculptor Christopher Frost began to ponder what it meant for such a diverse set of individuals to end up side by side. He posed a novel question: did the graves of the deceased match the style of their houses in life?

The result is "Neighbors" – a sculptural installation comprised of eight miniaturized facsimiles of the former homes of eight current residents of Forest Hills Cemetery. Frost selected the dead to reflect different classes, professions, and times. He used the cemetery archives and other historical records to pinpoint addresses and source images of historic homes, then went to the studio.

Of his vision, Frost said, "I wanted the buildings to form a little 'village,' creating a kind of community." Indeed, tucked up onto a rocky outcropping, coated in moss and shaded by overhanging leaves, the eight cast-concrete replicas look like an abandoned outpost of Fraggle Rock. The buildings' architectures vary dramatically, from the square and modernist to the elegantly ornate. (Note the very fetching mansard roof, complete with tower.)

Frost chose not to identify the owners of the homes on the sculptures, electing instead to label them by profession: "Merchant," "Grocer," "Architect," "Lead Manufacturer." Over a decade later, he's willing to reveal some of his sources: "'Poet' was Anne Sexton, 'Wagon Driver' was Cesarean Nicolo who died in the Great Molasses Flood, 1919."

The sculptor seems frankly overjoyed that the work continues to exist: "This was meant to be a temporary piece, installed for one year. Forest Hills asked to keep it. I said yes. Where else would it go?"

The same, of course, could be said of the homes' owners.

# GRAVE OF PIETRO CAPRONI

*Copies of two lions from the tomb of
Pope Clement XIII's at the Vatican*

*95 Forest Hills Avenue*
*Visit foresthillscemetery.com for open hours*
*Orange Line/Forest Hills*

Forest Hills Cemetery was designed as a park as much as a final resting place. This is fitting, as Forest Hill – established in 1848 – is of a piece with Boston's "Emerald Necklace."

Among the famous folks interred here – including poet e.e. cummings and several Massachusetts governors – is an artist named Pietro

Caproni. Caproni had a highly specific talent, ideal for the norms of the late 19th and early 20th centuries: he was a maker of plaster casts and copies of works from antiquity, especially Greek, Roman, and Egyptian originals. In an age before accessible photography, plaster casting and reproductions were a common way for museums and individuals to build their collections.

Pietro and his brother had a thriving business based on their direct access to European art: they created casts directly from original pieces at the Louvre, the Vatican, the Uffizi, and the British Museum, including the Elgin Marbles. In Boston, the brothers produced 16 casts of Greek and Roman subjects related to literature and music for the opening of Symphony Hall in 1900. Antiquity wasn't their only subject: their company P.P. Caproni and Brother also produced miniature versions of the North End's Paul Revere statue.

Pietro passed away in 1928 and left a specific request: he wanted his tomb to have – what else? – copies from a more famous tomb!

Pietro specifically requested copies of two lions from the tomb of Pope Clement XIII at the Vatican. The majestic lions are the work of an 18th century Venetian sculptor named Antonio Canova and were once quite well known. For a time, Caproni's company sold miniatures of them.

In the original, one lion slumbers peacefully while the other looks on protectively. (It is said they represented the Pope's vigor and moderation.) On Pietro's tomb, they've been realigned and the wakeful lion is staring off into the distance while the sleeper faces away. They look like a couple in the throes of an argument.

Still, the artistry in the manes and musculature is stellar. They're well worth a copy.

---

"Boy in the Boat" is another notable, though grisly, grave: a cherubic young boy grasping a tennis racket and a shell is stepping out of a boat. The boy is five-year-old Louis Mieusset, who would drown moments later, attempting to save his pet rabbit.

# BONSAI AND PENJING COLLECTION

*A little fairy place*

*Harvard's Arnold Arboretum*
*125 Arborway – 5-minute walk from Centre Street Gate*
*Select Thursday and Sunday, May–October, 11am–1pm*
*Orange Line/Forest Hills*

Opened in 1872, Harvard's Arnold Arboretum is a 281 acre "living museum" of trees, flowers, shrubs, and other flora. The park is a legal oddity: in 1882, in need of funds, Harvard and Boston struck a deal that the land would become part of the city's park system and stay open to the public if Boston would provide maintenance and security. Harvard maintained operational control. The agreement is technically a 1,000-year lease, renewable once. (The year 3882 may prove a contentious one.)

The arboretum is home to both serious scientific study and the simple appreciation of natural beauty. Of its 15,500 individual plants, the 43 residents of the Bonsai and Penjing Collection stand out for their striking profiles and rich cultural history.

In 1937, Larz Anderson, former U.S. Ambassador to Japan, died, and his wife donated his collection of Japanese dwarfed trees. Additional trees followed, along with funds for their care. Anderson's passion for bonsai suffuses his personal journals of Japan: "About us were dwarf trees of fantastic shape and stunted plum in fragrant bloom, white and pink, and gnarled trees of hundreds of years old…Isabel and I stopped so long in this little fairy place."

© Tiffany Enzenbacher / Arnold Arboretum of Harvard University

Six of Anderson's compact hinoki cypresses remain the centerpiece of the collection and astound for their age, ranging from 145 to 270 years old. Harvard is also experimenting with bonsaiing nontraditional plants from the arboretum's many species.

Bonsai and penjing are the Japanese and Chinese aesthetic practices of potting, pruning, wiring, and arranging trees of various species to attain a graceful miniaturized form. The Chinese art predates bonsai by thousands of years; the Japanese practice likely developed out of penjing when the countries opened diplomatic relations in the 7th century.

The collection is stored in a custom-built hexagonal lath house that allows for shading and air circulation. During the harsh winter months, the plants are moved into protective cold storage and held between 34 and 38 degrees Fahrenheit. The park also installed a security system after six bonsai were stolen in 1986.

## Leaves used to make wreaths for Boston Marathon competitors

The collection also includes an olive tree sourced from Mount Olympus. Its leaves have been used to make wreaths for Boston Marathon competitors.

## Extinct in the wild

Today, the arboretum systemically preserves species that are threatened by climate change and habitat loss. But in a few cases, the "living museum" also got lucky. If you walk along the Chinese Path on the southwest side of Bussey Hill, you will come upon Franklinia alatamaha, sprawling trees that resemble giant shrubbery. (Their droopy branches serve an evolutionary purpose: where they touch the ground, new trees will grow.)

This is the Franklin Tree, a native of south Georgia and extinct in the wild since 1803. The tree was first discovered by John Bartram, who was named by King George III as his official "Botanist in North America." Bartram was a Pennsylvanian and decided to name the plant in honor of his friend and founding father, Benjamin Franklin. Bartram's son collected seeds of the Franklin Tree and cultivated them in Philadelphia; Harvard's are the oldest documented specimens in the world.

*Cars in the Carriage House*

15 Newton Street
Tuesday–Sunday 10am–3pm
Orange Line/Forest Hills

In 1897, Larz Anderson, a Harvard man and career diplomat, married Isabel Weld Perkins, and they were a match for the ages. Both were well-born, well-connected, and well-moneyed, Isabel especially: she inherited a fortune from her shipping magnate grandfather, William Fletcher Weld, when she was just 5 years old.

Larz and Isabel traveled extensively, hosted society events, and shared a passion for the newest innovation at the time: horseless carriages. Their first purchase was an 1899 Winton Phaeton, one of just 100 made by the Winton Motor Carriage Company, a former bicycle-making operation. The Phaeton uses a tiller to steer, like a boat.

The Andersons averaged about a car a year for the next few decades, topping out at 32 in the collection. As they would retire or upgrade each vehicle, the Andersons would park the cars in the French chateau-inspired Carriage House at Weld, their Brookline home. Thus began America's oldest car collection. The museum still occupies the Carriage House, and Weld's land is now the Larz Anderson Park. The Phaeton is on permanent display.

The collection preserves 14 of the Andersons' cars, including a 1901 40-horsepower racer called a Winton Bullet – one of only four made, and the only one that survives. The Andersons were no strangers to alternative energy: they had a steam-powered 1903 Gardner-Serpollet (which came equipped with a summer body and a winter body that could be swapped to match the weather) and two electric vehicles, including Isabel's favorite, a 1908 Bailey Electric Phaeton Victoria. (Isabel was the first woman in Massachusetts to get a driver's license.)

The cars have wonderfully evocative nicknames, including a 1915 Packard Twin Six known as "12 Apostles" for its 12-cylinder engine.

While the cars are the stars of the show, the museum also preserves carriages and sleighs, plus the Ralph W. Galen Collection of Historic Bicycles and the papers of the defunct Packard Motor Car Company.

## "Lawn Events"

It is particularly joyful to attend one of the museum's themed "Lawn Events" in the warmer months. Automobile buffs and collectors are welcome to drive directly on the park's vast lawns, trailers in tow, to show off their favorite rides. Themes may be geographic (German, Italian, Swedish), scientific (alternative fuels), or highly specific (Extinct Car Day.)

# JAMAICA POND BENCH

*Unsittable seating*

507 Jamaicaway
Green Line/Heath Street

Jamaica Pond teems with people out for a jaunt, but few notice that among the many benches surrounding the pond, there is a practical joker – a bench that mimics its neighbors… save for a place to actually sit down.

Its creator, Matthew Hinçman, is an artist and JP resident. In 2005, he was examining the ubiquitous benches when, "In my mind's eye, I was using a mirroring tool to picture what those benches could be – they could be a kayak, a canoe, a cradle." Inspired, he tracked down Herwig Lighting, the Arkansas-based manufacturer of the pond's metal "Victoria" benches, and persuaded a manager to sell him two benches for $5,000. He cut, positioned, and welded the bench backs together to realize the mirrored image he had dreamed up.

At 5am on a rainy day in 2006, Hinçman and some friends snuck into the park and got to work. At the end of a row of identical benches, they laid down heavy slabs of steel and bolted the bench into place, then drove spikes into the ground and covered the base with dirt. They then disappeared into the dark and waited for the guerilla art to be discovered.

"It took a couple of weeks to be noticed," Hinçman remembers – even though he had attached a small plastic pocket on the bench to hold a card with his name and address. In place, the bench was so convincing that the few who did notice it figured it came from City Hall.

In time, the Parks Department realized it was unsanctioned and removed it. The Head of Facilities was so impressed by the workmanship he encouraged Hinçman to get permission for reinstallation. Within two months, Hinçman received approval by the Boston Art Commission.

Though Hinçman has experienced several rounds of removal and reinstallation since, the bench is back and has earned a cult following. A local nonprofit mailed a holiday card showing it loaded with presents. Someone installed a fabric top to transform it into a covered wagon. At least one proud JP resident has a tattoo of the bench. "Same-sex couples love to take engagement photos on it – two of the same object, mushed together," Hinçman notes.

With a laugh, he recounts the many names he has heard for it over the years: the Taco Bench, the U Bench, the Celery Bench. "People think it looks like a coffin or a joint roller or a cigarette roller. All these wacky things sit adjacent to it."

Yet no one sits comfortably on it.

# DODECAGONAL HOUSE

*12 sides and one mystery*

*17 Cranston Street*
*Orange Line/Jackson Square*

The historic house sitting atop a small mound once known as Cedar Hill defies logic: it is dodecagonal – that is, 12-sided. The application for the home to join the National Register of Historic Places notes: "its format defies classification in traditional building terms."

When Bob Field moved into the house in 1996, he noted that hexagons kept popping up. Underneath the house's modern siding was its original exterior from the 1870s: carefully crafted six-sided wooden shingles that fit perfectly together, creating a honeycomb effect. (These are visible today.) The house has numerous custom stained-glass windows, each home to a glass hexagon. Its six-sided cupola is topped with a six-sided skylight.

Even the twelve walls are derived from hexagons: viewed from above, the house is constructed as three vertical hexagonal columns, joined at the middle of the house

Field was determined to figure out who built the house and why. The mortgage records named John and Archibald Scott as the owners of the land. Archibald, an immigrant from Nova Scotia, worked at an organ factory nearby – a profession that, some posited, might lead one to build unconventionally, with a focus on upright columns. Field visited Nova Scotia to learn more.

But as he dug deeper into the historical record, the story grew complicated. A 1908 article from the *Boston Daily Globe* noted the "most peculiar and interesting house" was built by "two brothers from Scotland...which they intended should be used for their bachelor apartments." After revisiting his research, Field realized his trip to Nova Scotia might have been a mistake: in Boston, in 1871, there were TWO Archibald Scotts – one a married organ maker, one a single carpenter – living just blocks from each other.

At least that's one theory. Field hypothesizes the two Archibalds might have been the same man registering differently at two locations, maybe a home and a workshop. Maybe John was not his brother but his fellow homebuilder, and maybe neighbors mistook them for brothers.

And the hexagons? Field has an idea there, too. Maybe John Scott was in fact a Scottish immigrant to the U.S. and took inspiration from Fingal's Cave on the coast of Scotland, where basalt rock forms in perfect six-sided columns.

It's a lot of maybes.

# NIRA ROCK

*Metropolitan mountaineering*

*22 Nira Avenue*
*Orange Line/Jackson Square*

**B**oston maintains a program that selects so-called "urban wilds" for protection: small pockets of nature crammed in between the city's businesses and homes and meant to preserve some sense of what the area was like in the pre-industrial age.

The most distinctive of the urban wilds is Nira Rock, a 40 foot cliff face on which visitors can rock climb, whether by top-roping using permanent anchors embedded in the rock or (the more harrowing option) ropeless bouldering.

In the 19th century, this area was farmland and the outcropping was known as "Bleiler's Ledge." The rock itself is composed of smaller pebbles from rivers that, over millennia, became cemented together, giving a mottled appearance to the ledge. Early Massachusetts settlers thought the rock looked like traditional English Christmas pudding studded with bits of fruit and dubbed it, appropriately, "puddingstone."

Boston's neighbor, Roxbury, in fact, derived its name from "Rocksberry," in honor of the area's distinctive minerals, and Roxbury Puddingstone has been honored by the legislature as the official rock of the Commonwealth of Massachusetts. The stone's toughness and attractiveness made it a desirable building material, and quarries soon displaced the farms. An 1896 annual report from the City's Street Department notes: "A new crushing plant was built at Bleiler's Ledge on Heath Street" after rock quality nearby was deemed disappointing.

Today, you can spy local puddingstone used throughout the city's Olmsted parks, the Boston College campus, and many historic sites including Brattle Square Church. (see p. 180)

While the demand for puddingstone eventually cooled, it revved back to life in 1933 thanks to a Depression-era federal program called the National Industrial Recovery Act – NIRA. The name stuck even once the quarries had again been shuttered.

In the 1980s, the neglected site was rehabilitated through a number of nonprofits, government agencies, and private actors. (REI is responsible for the permanent anchors.)

## *Apples, pears, plums, and berries for free*

While the bravest souls experience the park vertically, an organization called The Friends of Nira Rock also maintains a small orchard and visitors are free to try its apples, pears, plums, and berries.

It can be a jarring experience for urban dwellers to pass by midday and see their neighbors dangling above.

# WATERWORKS MUSEUM

*Engineering marvels saved*

*2450 Beacon Street*
*Wednesday–Sunday 11am–4pm; Saturday 10am–3pm*
*Closed Monday and Tuesday*
*Green Line/Chestnut Hill Avenue or Cleveland Circle or Reservoir*

Next to the Chestnut Hill Reservoir, in a High Victorian building that is more European church than New England municipal utility, the Waterworks Museum protects engineering wonders: three towering 19th century water pumps that kept Boston hydrated even as demand ballooned with the population, which was nearly doubling every 20 years.

At its height, this pumping station daily moved 100 million gallons of water uphill to the Fisher Hill reservoir, where gravity pulled it down to Boston. Pride of place is given to the Leavitt Triple Expansion Engine, a three-cylinder behemoth installed in 1894 and named for creator Eramus B. Leavitt, a steam engine expert and designer of U.S. Navy ships. He was a founding member of the American Society of Mechanical Engineers, which declared the pump a National Historic Mechanical Engineering Landmark in 1973.

The Leavitt Engine was the second to be added to the building, but posed a problem: its immense scale could not fit in the existing structure. Leavitt found a solution: he dug a pit and lowered the pumps below and behind the pistons they would power, which was novel but awkward. The complexity shortened the life of the engine (it functioned until 1928), but also made it one of the most efficient engines of its time.

The other engines in the space are impressive if less distinctive in design. The Allis, added in 1898, required an addition to the original station and outperformed the Leavitt. Great arches beautifully frame the Allis. An elegant spiral staircase stands at one corner. Visitors can check out the upper levels on special tours. The Allis remained in service until 1976, when steam-powered pumps were decommissioned.

Despite the scale of these machines, crews were small, usually just one or two engineers, an oiler, a fireman, and a cleaner. The museum notes that the men became so accustomed to the sound of the smooth-running pumps that they depended on their ears to diagnose malfunctions.

As you leave, crane your neck and look high up at the front face of the Waterworks's tower: architect Arthur Vinal carved his own mustachioed visage and his wife Ada's dowdy face into cornerstones near the roof.

# BOSTON COLLEGE LABYRINTH

*The longest path*

*In front of the John J. Burns Library*
*191 College Road*
*Green Line/Chestnut Hill*

I n 2003, Boston College installed a massive labyrinth into the ground in front of the John J. Burns Library. The installation is a memorial for the 22 BC alumni who died in the events of 11 September 2001 and remains a peaceful place for contemplation and prayer.

Oddly, the labyrinth is a direct copy of the maze laid in the floor of the nave of Chartres Cathedral, likely between 1215 to 1221.

Labyrinths were a common feature of European churches of the Middle Ages and awash in symbolism. The mazes have been interpreted in many ways, including as the circuitous route pilgrims must take to reach the Holy Land or the journey Jesus made through hell before ascending to heaven or the path humans take through life to reach salvation.

The great circular perimeter is thought to represent the wholeness of Creation in God, and the cross in the center of the Chartres design is a clear reference to the Holy Cross and and Christianity's belief that following Jesus's teachings is the one truth path. In fact, the Chartres labyrinth is unicursal, meaning there is only one path to its center, and that path is the longest way.

The labyrinth is 50 feet wide, with the names of the deceased alumni carved into the outer edge. At its dedication ceremony, BC's president reflected, "May this labyrinth, influenced by the faith of medieval pilgrims, built in loving memory, dedicated today in prayer and community, forever be a place of healing, consolation, and peace. May its presence on the Boston College campus call us to understand that even in darkness, there is a path on which we can walk. Even in confusion there is grace to guide our journey. And even when we seem to stand most distant from where we began, we can yet turn again toward home, moving according to the sure compass of God's enduring love."

If you're in need of further contemplation, Wellesley College offers an alternative with an environmental spin: in 2017, students constructed a labyrinth out of large sections of downed trees and branches from around campus, including an impressive central slab from a 130 foot beech tree planted by Wellesley founder Henry Durant.

*Preserving a people*

*65 Main Street*
*Thursday–Sunday 12pm–6pm*
*Not easily accessible via public transport*

Watertown is home to one of the largest populations of Armenian immigrants in the U.S., as confirmed by its markets abounding in hummus, eggplant, and borek (cheese-stuffed pastries.) Many residents trace their roots to relatives who escaped the mass killing of Armenians by the Ottoman Empire from 1915 to 1917 during World War I, a history the museum movingly preserves.

In 1985, the Armenian Museum of America opened in the basement of The First Armenian Church of Belmont, with a mission to celebrate the culture of Armenia through books and objects. In 1988, the museum renovated a former bank, which today holds a sleek set of galleries displaying the treasures of the collection, ranging from ancient coins to traditional musical instruments to expertly woven rugs.

The museum's religious holdings underline the importance of the Armenian Church in protecting the culture of a people who have for centuries been fighting against neighbors, be they Persian, Byzantine, Arab, or Ottoman. Armenia lays claim to being the first Christian nation, having named Christianity the state religion in 301 AD. The first Bible printed in the Armenian language was made in Amsterdam circa 1666 by Oskan Erevants'i and is beautifully preserved here. There's also a flabellum – a fabulously decorated metal disc used to fan insects away from the holy wine and Eucharist during ceremonies – and a fetching container for chrism, "a mixture of the oils of 40 to 48 flowers, purified olive oil, and balsam...prepared once every five to seven years...and then distributed to all Armenian churches worldwide." The container is shaped like a bird and the oil is poured out through its beak.

Other highlights include a 630-pound khachkar, a type of stylized cross Armenians have been carving since the 9th century and consider a symbol of their heritage.

The museum movingly recounts the Armenian genocide through objects, many saved by those who managed to escape. An enormous 80-pound copper tray was saved by "a man named Garabedian," who strapped it to his back and climbed across the Taurus Mountains. On display is a model of a traditional home that was crafted from the memories of an Armenian immigrant. When he arrived in the U.S, the man searched out an Armenian-American who lived in Worcester, and declared to him, "I lived in your grandfather's home as a boy." He then described the house in great detail. That vivid description became the basis for the museum's model.

# PONYHENGE

*An unstable stable*

*Old Sudbury Road, near intersection with Appletree Lane*
*Not easily accessible via public transport*

Despite its proximity to Boston, Lincoln's vibe is decidedly rural. Amid the farmland, gardens, and real-life grazing animals, however, an unexpected herd stands out: a large collection of mismatched rocking horses in various states of functionality and disrepair.

Dubbed "Ponyhenge" by social media users for its remote location and oddly somber, supernatural aura, the collection is the creation of Lincoln residents Elizabeth Graver and Jimmy Pingeon, who moved their family's rocking horse out to the field in 2010 or 2011 when their daughters had outgrown it. A second rocking horse soon showed up unannounced. A third followed, and on and on until a discarded-toy herd was established. Graver and Pingeon unwittingly found themselves the caretakers of an ever-fluctuating number of rocking horses of all sorts — metal and wooden, large and tiny, handmade and mass manufactured, near-new and near-disintegrated.

Graver has come to consider Ponyhenge "an accidental piece of evolving folk art." Visitors donate their keepsakes and take home toys for their little ones. They rearrange the horses and stage scenes; as the Ponyhenge name suggests, an arrangement of two concentric circles is a popular option.

For a time, people would leave letters and prayers in a wooden box embedded into one of the resident ponies. People have shown up for visits bedecked in full cowboy regalia. A couple got married with the horses as witnesses. Others have dressed up the horses in finery – hats, ribbons – to celebrate the Kentucky Derby and wrapped them in lights for Christmas. A rocking duck appeared and was allowed to remain (after some debate). Carousel horses and antique pieces have come and gone.

A visit to Ponyhenge is striking for the site's eerie but joyful atmosphere. The toys stand silent yet animated, some with alert eyes and horsey smiles and some sun-bleached and rusted. The juxtaposition of childhood fantasy and the real-world grind couldn't be clearer.

Graver and Pingeon ask two things of visitors: please don't park on the grass or in the driveway, and please do take a horse with you if you can give it a good home.

# WATER SYSTEM TERRAZZO FLOOR MAP

*A celebration of sewers*

Cambridge Water Department
250 Fresh Pond Parkway
Monday 8:30am–8pm, Tuesday–Thursday 8:30am–5pm, Friday 8:30am–12pm
Red Line/Davis

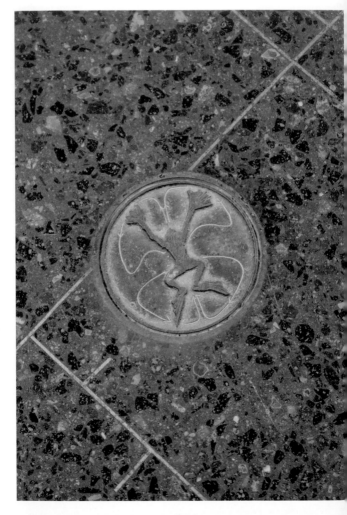

The Cambridge Water Department is not your typical municipal building. It is positioned on the shores of the beautiful Fresh Pond – the holding reservoir for the city's water supply – and incorporates architecture, sculpture, and art to educate locals about the infrastructure that keeps their taps running.

The artists Mags Harries and Lajos Héder dreamed up the multidimensional artwork. On a walking path around the reservoir you'll find a whimsical water fountain – fittingly called "The Squirt" – which is shaped like a gushing burst of H2O and seems to draw from a giant pipe directly out of the processing facility. An 11-foot water column inside the lobby bubbles and lights up when a pedestrian stops for a sip, connecting the drink to the purification process that happens within the facility's walls. A large black metal circle in the fence that surrounds the reservoir frames an idyllic scene of water, foliage, and lazily floating fowl – a real-world tableau demonstrating that human infrastructure doesn't have to mean industrial eyesores. The circle isn't just a frame – it's a slice of a 42-inch water main cheekily transformed into a viewing station.

The extent of the city's infrastructure comes to life most compellingly inside the building. During regular hours, visitors can enter the spacious Water Department Lobby and browse a 2,500 square foot terrazzo floor map that shows the pipes that run underground to feed homes, pools, fountains, and natural water features. Visitors are left with an impression of a massive hidden web pumping away just below our feet and sustaining modern standards of living.

Inset on the map are 15 bronze medallions that show scenes related to water – a scuba diver, children splashing, snowflakes. Each of these medallions has a large-scale counterpart in the form of a water valve cover embedded in the sidewalk adjacent to a Cambridge public school, thus inviting students to think more deeply about the water system.

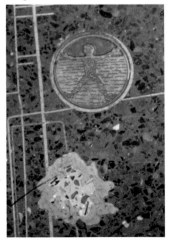

Seats around the lobby are made from water pipes of various diameters, giving visitors a better sense of scale and the chance to touch – and sit on – conduits that are usually hidden from view.

# THE "GLOVE CYCLE" ARTWORK

*In honor of lost gloves*

*Porter Square Station*
*Red Line/Porter*

At 105 feet below street level, the Porter Square Station is the lowest subway platform in the transit system. The escalators stretch downward ominously. As they ride, astute passersby note stray gloves on the partitions separating the escalators, just over from the railings.

The gloves – actually bronze sculptures – are in various states, some seemingly accidentally left behind, others stuck on anti-sliding knobs, still others splayed helplessly. The specificity of each glove starts to make them seem almost organic – little creatures worthy of a Pixar film, far from home and wondering what plot twist comes next.

This is "The Glove Cycle," an artwork installed by Mags Harries in 1984 as part of an MBTA program to beautify its stations.

There are 54 gloves spread throughout the station, each cast using the lost wax method, save the totally flattened ones, which were sandcast. While the gloves are stationary, physics does seem to apply to their story: as the escalators near their bottom and even out, many more gloves are gathered in heaps. (Mags once overheard a blind person say he used the density of gloves to forewarn him when he needed to step off the escalator.)

On the floors, the gloves are smashed flat, mangled, swept into tall piles in a corner. These most desperate gloves most powerfully evoke those that inspired Mags to create the work. In 1978, following a blizzard, Mags was walking through Radcliffe Yard and noted a lost glove someone had stuck atop a pole – "that was an ahha moment," she says. As the snow melted, she went out searching for more lost gloves, mapping their positions and collecting them. Mags noted how the gloves "were all squashed and sodden in different ways," seemingly animated. It was a sculptor's dream.

A close study of the work reveals characters, allusions, and hidden dramas. A child's alligator glove tells a different story than a workman's glove. Some have spotted a cheeky reference to the Sistine Chapel's "The Creation of Adam" as two gloves stretch toward each other, fingers extended, not quite touching. One can only guess why some gloves seem to have only three fingers, poor things.

Mags delights in the ways normal people interact with her creations: she has seen money and Hershey Kisses placed in them, an open hand with an offering for the next tired commuter.

# HENDERSON CARRIAGE

*Real horsepower*

*2067–2089 Massachusetts Avenue*
*Lobby is accessible during normal business hours*
*Red Line/Porter*

In 1841, Robert Henderson set up shop as a blacksmith in North Cambridge. Over the ensuing years, he expanded the operation to include his two sons. In 1857, the Henderson Brothers Company was founded. They primarily manufactured horse-drawn carriages and became widely celebrated. According to the Cambridge Historical Society, the Henderson name was "nationally known not only for its brakes, drags, barges, and wagons, but also for its mail carriages, passenger carriages, sleighs, and caravans."

An 1892 fire destroyed the thriving enterprise, but the Hendersons immediately rebuilt bigger and better. The towering brick edifice at 2067 Mass Ave still bears the family name on its front, though it is now home to a preschool, medical office, and various shops. Head inside the back lobby and you'll see what it was all about: an antique Henderson carriage (sans horse) greets visitors and evokes that bygone era, even as the T rushes below and traffic streams up Mass Ave just beyond the building doors.

This carriage, built in 1892, was known as a Curtain Rockaway and features a number of innovations, including side curtains that could be drawn up to let air into the cab and a removable partition between the driver and the passengers. That the driver sat at the same level as the passengers in this model was considered a modern, "democratic" move.

The Henderson family eventually built three additional manufacturing facilities alongside this one, making it the second largest carriage factory in the United States. The building that stands today was the carriage repository. It held about 2,000 carriages in its top four floors.

Local legend has it that Francis Robert Henderson, the eventual owner of the business, turned down an offer from Henry Ford to convert the factories into a Ford plant, asserting, "The automobile is only a fad; the horse and buggy are here to stay."

It's a terrific story, but unverified – and undercut, perhaps, by the fact that the Hendersons did shift to producing truck bodies alongside traditional carriages in the 1910s. By the 1920s, the industry had passed them by and the company went under.

Irony of ironies: from 1929 to the early 1980s, the Henderson carriage repository – once the cutting-edge home of modern transportation – served as (you guessed it) a Ford car dealership.

# HONK! FESTIVAL

*Brassy bands*

*Davis Square*
*Visit honkfest.org for dates and performance schedule*
*Red Line/Davis*

For three days each October, Davis Square fills with the blare of trumpets, the rat-a-tat of snare drums, and the oompah of countless tubas. The players are clad in garish costumes of all make and manner, and the crowds hoot and holler for more.

The HONK! Festival takes its name from this happy din.

HONK! was started in 2006 as a gathering of so-called activist marching bands – bands of socially engaged political activists using music to connect with others and promote, in the words of HONK! organizers, "freedom, justice and collective emancipation." The HONK! showrunners are looking both to host a raucous weekend of concerts and to reclaim public spaces through art and grassroots community-building.

Come for da beats, stay for debates, essentially.

In keeping with its lefty politics, the festival is proudly non-commercial and the bands don't ascend any stages; their performances are at street-level and at close range to the audience. Jam sessions turn into dance parties unexpectedly.

The festival starts off on Friday with a nighttime parade, essentially a motley crew of enthusiastic (and possibly inebriated) musicians roving the streets with instruments, lanterns, and glow-sticks. The atmosphere is part Haunted House, part Mardi Gras. Saturday and Sunday feature performances in every nook and cranny of Davis Square and culminate in a parade down a nearly 2 mile stretch of Massachusetts Avenue to Harvard. Many of the bands and participants also find time to protest, perform at prisons, or lead roundtable discussions.

Each year, activist bands travel from around the world to join in HONK!, including Pakava It from Moscow, Russia; Banda Rim Bam Bum from Santiago, Chile; and the impressively named Bolschewistische Kurkapelle Schwarz-Rot from Berlin, Germany. In addition to their music, the bands often share messages about oppression, social justice, or other urgent political matters they're tackling back home.

The music styles range as widely as the political arguments. Around every corner, you might discover a pop classic, an oompah march, a hip hop jam, a salsa beat, or a jazz improv.

No matter your politics, it's best to just raise your fist and dance.

# MCLEAN MODEL

*Insane asylum on a pole*

*57 Davis Square*
*Red Line/Davis*

In a park by the Davis T stop, metal poles are topped by colorful if weather-beaten sculptures that symbolize Somerville's "Seven Hills" and the industries that established the city. There's a cow for the dairies, an apple tree for the orchards, a fish for the maritime trades...and, bizarrely, a stately-looking dollhouse of the original "McLean Asylum for the Insane."

The city's seven hills – Cobble, Spring, Winter, Clarendon, Ploughed, Prospect, Central – are gone. Ploughed and Cobble were carted away as landfill. Still, they loom large in local imaginations.

In the 1800s, the hills were pastoral and calm, an escape from the bustle of Boston. In 1816, the Massachusetts General Hospital Corporation bought 18 acres and the home of deceased businessman John Barrell. Barrell's mansion was constructed in 1792 by architect Charles Bulfinch, who was rehired to adapt the house into a hospital, with two new wings for mentally ill patients. Bulfinch toured hospitals in New York, Philadelphia, and Baltimore "to observe their construction and get a knowledge of their expenses and management."

Barrell's estate included terraces and fruit trees; a natural setting was considered ideal for treatment of mental illness.

When it opened in 1818, with space for 60 patients, the asylum was New England's first such hospital. Despite precautions – secured windows, bolted doors – patients escaped with frequency. Hospital board meetings record that "several elopements from the Asylum had occurred."

In 1826, the asylum was renamed for a donor. Despite its renown, in the decades that followed urban sprawl encroached upon the hill's tranquility; by 1872, two railroads ran straight through the McLean's grounds. The buildings, too, lost their polish. In 1851, a historian noted of the facilities, "[T]here are in them so many dark passages, so many ascents and descents, and so many turnings and twistings, that, should the oldest Trustee of the institution be suddenly left alone during a visit, he would probably be puzzled to know exactly where he was, or by what means he could best escape from the labyrinth around him."

In 1895, the hospital was moved to Belmont on a site chosen by Frederick Law Olmsted. The original McLean was razed in 1896, but its grand staircase is still viewable at the Somerville Museum.

# BATHTUB MARYS

*Renovations in reverence*

*Viewable at various locations around Somerville; notable example at*
*217 Powder House Boulevard*
*Red Line/Davis*

If you take the time to amble around Somerville's streets for more than a few blocks, you will notice an unusual tradition: residential front yard shrines featuring Catholic saints placed in old bathtubs.

Known to locals as "Bathtub Marys," the practice dates to the late 1940s and was popularized by the large Catholic immigrant communities in the area. Local experts believe the original shrine-makers were Portuguese immigrants in Fall River, MA (about an hour from Boston) who, while upgrading their homes to modern showers and bathroom fixtures, decided to reuse their old appliances – sometimes including claw-footed tubs – as the backdrop for public religious displays. Irish and Italian immigrants emulated the tradition, and the count in Somerville is estimated at 600 Bathtub Marys.

True to the moniker, the Virgin Mary is the most popular subject for the shrines, which echo popular Church iconography of Mary standing inside a grotto as "Our Lady of Lourdes," referencing miraculous appearances Mary reportedly made to believers in a cave in Lourdes, France.

But other saints are also regularly featured in Bathtub Mary displays, notably Saint Francis (identifiable by his signature brown robe and friendly birds), Saint Fiacre (patron saint of gardens, typically with a shovel), and Jesus himself.

A number of academics have studied Bathtub Marys and theorized about their historical meaning and persistence. Some believe that Bathtub Marys were placed in the front yards – rather than the more private backyards – to signal pride in home ownership, achieving the so-called "American Dream." Others believe that the flowers and greenery that often surround the shrines injected a bit of nature into cold, urban, cement-filled neighborhoods.

That they survive in today's increasingly secular context is a miracle worthy of Mary herself.

---

Beginning in 2012, a local librarian named Cathy Piantigini systematically traversed Somerville's streets to document Bathtub Marys. Her photos and street addresses are available at:
bathtubmarysofsomerville.tumblr.com.

# THE POWDER HOUSE

*From powder to pickles*

*Intersection of Broadway and College Avenue*
*Red Line/Davis*

The squat tower perched atop a small incline within Nathan Tufts Park holds two historical distinctions: it is the oldest stone building in Massachusetts and one of the first sites of British aggression in the lead-up to the Revolutionary War.

The building was constructed in 1704 by a French refugee and shipwright named Jean Maillet. He used it as a windmill. Local legend tells of a woman who ducked inside the windmill as she was being chased by an ill-intentioned man. The man became trapped in the workings of the mill and died.

In 1747, the Maillet family sold the building to the colony of Massachusetts, which removed the windmill blades and converted it into a storehouse for gunpowder. The building's 2 foot thick stone walls and high elevation made it an ideal place to protect the finicky munitions, which become ineffective in poor conditions.

In September 1774, tensions were high over the Intolerable Acts, a set of retaliatory taxes aimed at the colonists in the wake of the Boston Tea Party. Massachusetts Governor Thomas Gage became concerned when locals began taking gunpowder from the Powder House. He arranged to calmly take control of the key to the storehouse – but then lost patience and, aided by 260 British regulars, raided the stores instead. Some 250 barrels of gunpowder were confiscated by the government, an act that provoked the first mass demonstrations against British rule.

Seven months later, the Battles of Lexington and Concord kicked off the Revolutionary War, and the Powder House became the American Army's first munitions depot, serving George Washington's troops stationed up the road on Cambridge Common. Supplies were short for the colonists, and at one point the Powder House held just 38 kegs of powder.

In 1870, a Somerville resident named George Emerson opened a pickling facility in a shed near the tower. Emerson stored pickles in the cool interior of the Powder House and sold his wares as "Old Powder House Brand Pickles," complete with a drawing of the building on the label. It is rare to come across these antique pickle jars today, but on a walking path just downhill from the Powder House, there is a stone that seems to be littered with three bottles left over from teenage revelers the night before. Look closer: they are metal replicas of Emerson's pickle containers.

# MUSEUM OF MODERN RENAISSANCE

*Mythology on every wall*

*115 College Avenue*
*The museum welcomes visitors only sporadically. It can be visited most reliably during Somerville Open Studios*
*Visit somervilleopenstudios.org for dates and times*
*The artist-owners also open the house for musical performances and occasional tours throughout the year, usually announced on the museum's Instagram handle @museumofmod.renaissance*
*Red Line/Davis*

Nicholas Shaplyko and Ekaterina Sorokina describe themselves as "two artists with one soul," and their home is the embodiment of that soul: whimsical, joyful, life-affirming, riotous. Every surface in the house – which Shaplyko and Sorokina conceive of as a single work of art – is meticulously designed, with ceilings, walls, doors, and floors covered in mythological symbols from around the globe. The artist-owners open their home – which they call the Museum of Modern Renaissance – to the public on select dates throughout the year.

At every turn, visitors are greeted by gods and mystical creatures, kings and queens, angels and prophets, benevolent spirits and demons. Intricate patterns repeat and distort, framing scenes and merging spaces. Everything is painted in trippy-bright Technicolor.

Shaplyko and Sorokina emigrated from Russia to the United States as the Soviet Union collapsed in the 1990s. In 2002, the pair was searching for a building they could transform into a private home-*cum*-museum, a blank canvas. This former Masonic Lodge and Unitarian Church fit the bill, and for over a decade the artists painted, sculpted, and carved their vision into being.

From the street, it is clear this is no typical home. Above the main door sits the enormous sculpted face of a beast with bulging, heavily-lidded Muppet eyes and a bulbous nose. In warm months, a window box supplies flowery hair. Above, a stylized sun smiles serenely.

The entrance hall features a frieze entitled "The Parade of Planets," a panoply of zodiac symbols and Greco-Roman gods. A woman symbolizing the Moon rides atop a fearsome owl; Mercury nestles in a Celtic design; Venus emerges from sea foam while a pensive Neptune wields his trident. Mars, the god of war, is surrounded by foxes, the symbol of diplomacy. Two mirrors opposite one another offer a glimpse of infinity.

The centerpiece of the museum is the high-ceilinged Grand Hall, where Shaplyko and Sorokina host occasional musical and theatrical performances. Fifty-seven murals cover 5,200 square feet of wall space, straight up to the steepled ceiling. "This main hall is dedicated to myth, fairy tales, fables from different nations, different countries…myths of world creation. And some of them we just made up!" Nicholas notes.

Describing what he hopes visitors discover at his home, Nicholas grows reflective: "When you're looking at art and talk to it, you open the door to other dimensions and all of a sudden this other dimension is yourself. In normal everyday life, you don't have time to think about it…but art and meditation is a tool to go inside your own world and see why am I here? What am I doing here? Is it worth doing what I'm doing right now?"

# FRIEND SMITHSONIAN MUSEUM AND SAPPHIRE CITY

*Lost and found and fabulous*

*135 Highland Avenue*
*Red Line/Davis*

Retired teacher and Somerville resident Martha Friend has become locally famous for her found object art. Originally trained as a photographer, Friend found fulfillment in collecting the bric-a-brac of life – or, in her words, "flotsam and jetsam" – and reimagining it as artworks that burst with color and humor. While her unique brand of art may catch your eye in several places around Somerville (spot her diamond-studded forest diorama installed in a defunct telephone box in Davis Square), the most stunning treasures are on display outside Friend's home on Highland Avenue.

The yard is a riot of activity. Mysterious statues peek out from bushels of greenery. A small rusted altar – or is it an antique stove? – holds a sky blue Pegasus ready to take flight. The front porch, thick with light fixtures, is guarded by a driftwood ox with enormous horns.

Above the front steps, a hand-painted sign declares, "Dance Party." The roof above is packed with large, proud-looking toy horses, all painted a magnificent silver. Look closely and you'll spot tens of smaller figures engaged in whimsical stories of their own. On my visit, a red muscleman was doing splits while, nearby, a pea green dinosaur mauled a rhino.

Adjacent to the porch is a paradise of blue glass, which Friend titled "Sapphire City." Great stacks of deep blue glass objects seem to defy gravity. Friend acquired most of her material from thrift stores, though some were gifts or objects saved from the dump. In "Sapphire City," their curves and contours make it hard to decipher what each object was before it joined the assemblage – A lampshade? A vase? Is that a mold of a human hand? (It is.)

At the corner of the property sits a squat box with a clear front window. This is "The Friend Smithsonian Museum" – a tiny gallery featuring a rotating set of dioramas created by Friend and other artists. On my visit, the exhibit "Dinosaurs in Love" featured two bridal brachiosaurs ensconced in lace and, to their left, an ankylosaur smooching a stegosaur wearing extremely flirty lipstick.

According to Friend, she came up with the name for the museum "because my last name is Friend and my husband's last name is Smith and our children's last names are Friendsmith. Clever, huh?"

When pressed about where she draws inspiration, Friend responded with a simple truth her art makes undeniable: "Big plastic toys and spray paint are fun!"

# OBAMA ROSE GARDEN

*Mini garden for a major figure*

*365 Broadway Avenue*
*Green Line/Science Park-West End*

The Winter Hill neighborhood is typically associated with tales of the Irish Mafia and crime boss Whitey Bulger, but another famous leader called Winter Hill home for a short period: Barack Obama lived in a garden-level apartment in the brick edifice called Langmaid Terrace from 1988 to 1991.

In fact, when Massachusetts Governor Deval Patrick was leaving his position in 2014, the president called into Patrick's "Ask the Governor" radio segment on public radio and said, "Governor, this is Barack Obama, formerly of Somerville. I've got a few complaints about service in and around the neighborhood, but I've moved down South since that time."

Just in front of the former president's building, locals have created a rose garden in honor of the former tenant, along with a memorial plaque praising Obama's achievements while in office.

# HIDDEN EDSEL SYMBOL

## *Ford's forgotten flop*

*Set into a pillar in front of 698 Assembly Row*

Today, Somerville's Assembly Row neighborhood looks like an outlet mall peppered with bougie residential high-rises but, as its name suggests, this area was once an industrial center dominated by plants, machinery, and assembly lines.

In 1842, the Boston and Maine Railroad built rail connections here, and, in 1925, the opening of the McGrath Highway made the area attractive to industrial shipping. Factories sprang up on landfill, burying salty marshes along the Mystic River. In 1926, the quintessential American enterprise – Ford Motor Company – opened a massive 52 acre auto plant, giving the area its name. For a few decades, Assembly Row embodied the American Dream: a middle-class neighborhood close to good jobs with picnic areas along a picturesque river. From 1942 to 1945, the plant was redesigned to produce vehicles called "universal carriers" for the Allied Forces in World War II. It was the only plant in the U.S. to produce the troop carriers. In the 1950s, the Somerville plant was the only Ford factory devoted wholly to the "Edsel" – a line of cars (named for Henry Ford's son) which the company spent 10 years and $250 million developing. When the Edsel flopped in 1958, the factory doors closed.

A tribute to Ford's flop is hidden on a pillar outside Earl's restaurant at 698 Assembly Row: a stylized E in concentric circles – the infamous logo of the Ford Edsel.

# THE PLAQUE OF A DESTROYED CONVENT

*Violence spurred by a "mysterious lady"*

*To the right of the Somerville Library*
*115 Broadway*
*Orange Line/Sullivan Square*

"PLOUGHED HILL"
FORTIFIED AND BOMBARDED
IN 1775-76

SITE OF URSULINE CONVENT
FOUNDED 1820 AND OPENED 1826
BURNED 1834
HILL DUG DOWN 1875 TO 1897

ERECTED BY
MT. BENEDICT COUNCIL No. 75

S ite of Ursuline Convent
Founded and Opened 1826
Burned 1834"

That's how the Knights of Columbus chose to pithily summarize one of the most chilling anti-Catholic incidents in New England history, which took place atop Somerville's Ploughed Hill.

While today Boston is thought of as a Catholic town, the road to that reputation was long and violent. Waves of Irish immigration in the 1820s transformed the city, and local laborers – Protestant and uneducated – disliked the newcomers and their foreign ways.

Anti-Catholicism had a history in the state: the 1691 Charter of Massachusetts Bay called for religious freedom – except for Catholics: "Our heires and Successors Grant Establish and Ordaine that for ever hereafter there shall be a liberty of Conscience allowed in the Worshipp of God to all Christians (Except Papists)."

Nevertheless, the Church found a foothold and aimed to expand. In 1799, work began on a Catholic cathedral and in 1820 a school for girls was established by nuns of the Ursuline order. In 1826, Mother Superior Sister Mary Edmond St. George relocated the school to Ploughed Hill, soon to be renamed Mount Benedict in honor of the local bishop.

The building was a statement – perched atop a hill, three stories, large wings, elegant brick. There were classrooms, dorms, the bishop's house, terraced gardens. The statement was not missed by the increasingly disgruntled working class, who saw the Pope coming for New England. In the words of a student at the school, the convent "was as foreign as the soil whereon it stood, as if, like Aladdin's Palace, it had been wafted from Europe by the power of a magician."

Protestant preachers harangued against "Romish heretics" and rumors abounded. In July 1834, a local man was approached by an ill nun who had wandered from the convent. This encounter was spun into a tale of a "mysterious lady" being held against her will, which fueled talk of secret dungeons and torture chambers within the brick walls.

On 11 August, a large group of locals demanded to be let in to free the mystery captive. The Mother Superior spoke sharply, asserting the bishop had "twenty thousand of the vilest Irishmen at his command," which only fueled the mob's anger. Soon they breached the front doors and proceeded to smash windows, overturn furniture, and, ultimately, burn the great building. The nuns and students – likely about 60, many Protestant themselves – escaped through a back entrance.

The ruins remained for nearly 50 years, and several bricks were repurposed in the construction of the Cathedral of the Holy Cross in Boston.

# ELEPHANT ASHES

*A Jumbo jar*

*Tufts Office of the Director of Athletics*
*161 College Avenue*
*To arrange a time to visit, email john.morris@tufts.edu*
*Green Line/Medford-Tufts*

In 1884, P.T. Barnum – famous circus huckster – financed the building of the Barnum Museum of Natural History at Tufts University. Barnum was a trustee of the school, and the museum displayed his personal items and a number of taxidermied animals from the circus. In 1889, a showstopper joined the collection (after the entrance was widened): a 12 foot high, 1,500 pound African elephant named Jumbo.

Jumbo was famous for his size and his performances in the Barnum and Bailey Circus, though that was only the final stop of his busy life.

Captured in Abyssinia (today, Ethiopia) in 1861, he was sold to a collector of wild animals, who then sold the elephant to a small zoo in the Jardin des Plantes in Paris. After a period of illness, Jumbo was transferred to the London Zoo, where P.T. Barnum purchased him for $10,000. Jumbo arrived in the U.S. and performed in the circus from 1882 to 1885.

He was a sensation. Ever the marketer, Barnum told the *Philadelphia Press*, "I tell you, conscientiously, that no idea of the immensity of the animal can be formed. It is a fact that he is simply beyond comparison. The largest elephants I ever saw are mere dwarfs by the side of Jumbo." The world agreed: the word "jumbo" did not exist in the English language prior; it derives directly from the pachyderm.

As he was crossing a trainyard in Canada in 1885, Jumbo was struck and killed. Barnum preserved the bones and hide, touring both until 1889, when he gave the stuffed elephant to Tufts. (The bones went to the American Museum of Natural History in New York City.)

For over 80 years, Jumbo stood in Barnum Hall. He adopted as the Tufts mascot; students would tug on his tail and put pennies in his trunk for good luck. The wear took its toll, and Jumbo's tail had to be replaced; the original is kept in a Tufts archive.

Then, in April 1975, an electrical fire destroyed the building – and Jumbo. While the elephant's memory lives on in the form of a life-size statue on campus, few realize the ashes of the elephant were collected by an administrative assistant in the athletic department. She had on hand a peanut butter jar, in which the ashes still remain today. Visitors can find it on a shelf in the Office of the Athletic Director; the yellowing label reads, "Enclosed ashes are remains of Tufts' Jumbo lost in a fire at Barnum Museum on 4-14-75."

# SLAVE QUARTERS OF THE ROYALL HOUSE

*Last slave quarters in the North*

*15 George Street*
*Open only in summer and fall*
*Visit royallhouse.org/visit/hours-and-admission/ for dates and tour times*
*Green Line/Medford-Tufts*

In the 18th century, the Royalls were the largest slave-holding family in Massachusetts. From 1737 to 1781, over 60 enslaved people worked inside the mansion and in the family's 500 acres of fields. Today's museum preserves the three-story Georgian mansion and freestanding slave quarters – the only such structure in the American North.

The mansion was built by Isaac Royall off the profits of the family's highly lucrative sugar cane plantations in Antigua. When Royall relocated to Massachusetts, he brought an initial crew of 27 slaves with him.

The mansion has been open to the public as a museum since 1908, and visitors experience what fine living was like in the mid-1700s – ornamented woodwork, Delft-tiled fireplaces, lush textiles. Though the house is frozen in its pre-Revolution state, Royall fled these opulent surroundings for Canada at the start of the war, and colonial forces occupied these rooms. It's said George Washington even used the Marble Chamber as an interrogation room for British prisoners.

But the most extraordinary history preserved by the museum is the slave quarters 35 feet back from the main house. Most Americans are taught that slavery only existed in the southern states, with the North painted as a bastion of freedom. The narrow service staircase, with its deeply worn steps, tells a different story – one of tired feet, lack of choice, and endless toil.

Excavations at the site have turned up fascinating artifacts that make real the lives of the enslaved, including ceramic fragments and pieces of tile repurposed as marbles and game pieces. One can imagine children at leisure, just for a moment.

## Another reminder of Northern slavery

Another reminder of Northern slavery can be found along Grove Street, on the perimeter of Thomas Brooks Park. The Brooks family were wealthy slaveholders in the 1700s. When in 1924 the family donated this land to the city for the creation of a park, they stipulated "The Old Slave Wall" must be maintained. It dates to 1765 and is now known as "Pomp's Wall," in honor of its builder, an enslaved man named Pompeii. During restoration work, builders discovered clear hand- and fingerprints in the clay brick – likely the hand of Pompeii himself, still visible three centuries later.

# RUINS OF 1899 OBSERVATORY

*From cutting edge to lost*

*Middlesex Fells Reservation*
*Trail from Fellsway East in Melrose*
*No public transport available*

The Middlesex Fells Reservation covers 2,575 acres, hemmed in by highways and the sprawl of Greater Boston. Within its forests and rocky peaks, The Fells is home to what remains of a long-forgotten Geodetic Observatory built by MIT in 1899.

The institute had searched for a place to build a lab in the field for the study of geodetics – the science of measuring Earth's shape, size, and movement as well as the location of points all over the globe – which requires extreme precision, and thus distance from the effects of an urban environment like vibrations (caused by passing cars or trains), magnetic interference, or air and light pollution.

Further, geodetics work required the lab to be visible to other geodesic stations and, on top of the hill within The Fells, MIT's new building was in sight of U.S. Coast Geodetic Survey triangulation stations in Milton and Waltham.

The physical footprint was small – just 15 square feet – and the exterior was unpolished, with walls made of field stone from its surroundings. The roof had a gap to allow for direct observation of the sky and the ability to follow the meridian (a line of longitude) from one horizon to the other.

Despite its rough exterior, within were advanced scientific tools including a transit instrument telescope, sidereal chronometer, chronograph, and magnetometer, which allowed students to make magnetic and gravity observations and reliable measurements of longitude, latitude, and time.

Time, of course, is what reduced the observatory to its current tumbledown state – a fallen roof and walls in varying states of collapse. Exactly when MIT stopped using the station is a longstanding mystery. The institute built its Haystack Observatory in 1970, so it's likely the Middlesex Fells site was no longer needed after that point.

---

The reservation has about 20 miles of trails and getting to the Geodesic Observatory requires hiking on several of these paths. The shortest version is only about half a mile from a parking lot and has been informally dubbed the MIT Trail. You can find a clear guide atmaldenhistory.org/Fells/MIT/MIT-Trail.html.

---

# THE OLD SCHWAMB MILL

*Eccentric frames for eccentric people*

*17 Mill Lane*
*Tuesdays and Saturdays 10am–4pm*
*Not easily accessible via public transport*

In 1864, two German brothers named Charles and Frederick Schwamb joined forces to import to America a special woodworking craft: the carving of oval frames.

Their workshop has survived, with artisans doing exactly what they were doing 150 years ago, largely on the same equipment. The carving workshop has a ceiling covered with interconnected belts, pulleys, and shafts that, when fired up, power the machines below – saws, planers, boring machines, moulding machines, and the all-important lathes.

The lathes – machines that rotate wood so that craftspeople can use tools to shape it – were imported from Germany. They are known as "eccentric" lathes because they allow even eccentric – that is oval – shapes to be cleanly and evenly carved at significant speeds.

The brothers were sons of the Industrial Revolution and adopted new innovations, especially power sources. The original mill ran off an 18 foot waterwheel placed in a stream directly below the workshop. This was later supplemented with a steam engine and an 1888 Holyoke Hercules Turbine, which is still in the mill basement.

In the years immediately following the Civil War, photography became more accessible to the general public and black walnut frames with gold-leaf liners became all the rage. The Schwambs turned out thousands. The mill adjusted along with public tastes, adding a range of woods, finishes, and nearly endless grooves and profiles. Schwamb frames are in the collections of the White House, Buckingham Palace, and the Iolani Palace (the former home of the Hawaiian monarchy).

By 1969, the Schwamb family decided to sell the site to a trucking company. A local activist worked tirelessly to save the mill from demolition.

Today, the frames are crafted by a single wood turner, David Graf, and his craftsmanship is evident on every wall.

### "First snow Nov 13 – 1896"

The creaky mill shows its age. Keep your eye out for graffiti from former mill workers on the walls: "First snow Nov 13 – 1896" seems to have kicked off a tradition among subsequent generations. Also don't miss the glue room: every surface from table to ceiling is covered with 150-plus years' worth of hide-glue and its modern equivalents. When asked how such a heavy covering ended up on the ceiling, my guide laughed and said, "I have no idea!"

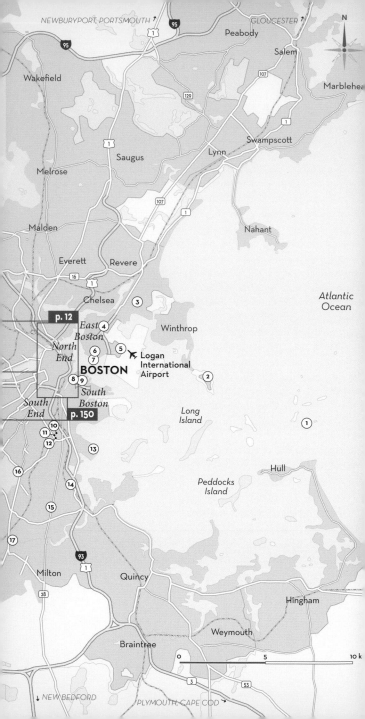

# *East*

# BOSTON LIGHT

*Last manned lighthouse*

*Tours depart from 191 West Atlantic Avenue*
*Visit bostonharborislands.org/lighthouse-tours to book a tour*
*Tours run only in warm weather months*
*Orange Line or Blue Line/State*

Little Brewster Island has been home to a lighthouse since 1716, when Massachusetts erected a 60 foot stone tower topped by a number of candles. In 1719, the colony added a fog cannon – the first fog signal in America. When ships entered Boston Harbor in poor weather, they would shoot a cannon and the lighthouse keeper would answer in kind, giving the captain some sense of his bearings.

Today the site is affectionately known as Boston Light. It bears two significant designations: it is the country's oldest continually running lighthouse and, by an odd stroke of legislation, its last manned lighthouse.

The building has been destroyed many times through the centuries, beginning in 1720 due to a fire caused by its own light. Storms and ocean conditions took their toll, and it was intentionally burned no less than four times during the Revolutionary War – thrice by patriots upset the lighthouse was under British control and once by the retreating British.

In 1809, when its walls began to crack, the government placed six iron hoops around the lighthouse like a metal girdle. The iron was eventually replaced by steel, which corroded. Today, five aluminum bands hug the structure tight.

From 1716 to present, maritime safety tech improved greatly, and Boston Light has been kept on the forefront. The fog cannon was replaced by a wind-up bell in 1851, then a whistle, a fog-trumpet, a steam siren, and finally a fog signal. (The fog cannon was returned to the island in 1993; it is the Coast Guard's oldest artifact.)

In time, the candles were replaced by lamps, first oil-fueled then electric. A revolving apparatus was added, then a reflector, and finally an epic piece of glasswork known as a Fresnel Lens. Installed in 1859, it is two solid tons of glass and stands 11 feet high. (The lighthouse had to be raised to 89 feet to accommodate it.) The lens concentrates the light into a single beam, which can be seen 27 miles out into the Atlantic Ocean.

In 1989, the Coast Guard was planning to automate the light completely, but Senator Ted Kennedy passed legislation through the U.S. Senate requiring Boston Light to be permanently manned. While the light was automated in 1998, a civilian keeper remains today to greet visitors and shed light on the site's rich history.

# DEER ISLAND DIGESTIVE EGG TOUR

## *Sewage with a view*

*190 Tafts Avenue*
*Call 617 660 7607 to book a tour*
*Free*
*Not easily accessible via public transportation*

The infrastructure that undergirds modern living is usually locked away from the public. Power stations, incinerators, sewers, subway control rooms, and the like are kept behind lock and key or buried out of sight.

The Deer Island Wastewater Treatment Plant in Boston Harbor is far from buried. In fact, the facility is often the first sight to greet tourists as they land at nearby Logan Airport.

What draws the attention of passengers?

The island's 12 gigantic industrial "eggs," each looming 10 stories high. These "eggs" are in fact 3 million gallon anaerobic digesters, home to millions of microbes munching on the sludgy sewage produced by over 2 million people living in Greater Boston. The bacteria consume much of the waste and, in the process, produce methane. The "eggs" are, essentially, 12 enormous stomachs.

Few realize that the Massachusetts Water Resources Authority offers free tours of the facility, including a visit to the buried bottoms and soaring tops of the eggs. As long as you don't mind the smell (yes, there is a smell), the catwalks connecting the digesters, 150 feet in the air, offer some of the city's best views of the harbor and the skyline. There is also a blessedly thick window that allows visitors to peer down into the eggs' stinky depths. In the words of my tour guide, that is where "the bugs get fat and happy."

The digesters are one component in the mind-bogglingly complex sewage cleaning process that has transformed Boston Harbor, historically one of the most polluted harbors in the country. Environmentalists wielding the Clean Water Act of 1972 pressured the city to invest in clean-up, and today's Deer Island is the result.

Pollutants are removed from water through a series of "grit chambers," "settling tanks," "disinfection basins," and, of course, the eggs. At certain points of the process, pure oxygen is pumped into the flow to promote the growth of microorganisms; at others, sodium hypochlorite kills the bacteria.

In the end, a 9.5 mile tunnel under the Atlantic Ocean whisks away the now-safe, treated sewage (called effluent) and deposits it into the depths of Massachusetts Bay.

After the tour, visitors can contemplate the engineering marvels they've seen on a breathtakingly beautiful 2.5 mile nature walk that surrounds the wastewater facility.

# MADONNA QUEEN
# OF THE UNIVERSE SHRINE

*Honoring an escape from Nazis in Italy*

*120 Orient Avenue*
*Tuesday–Sunday 9am–8pm*
*Blue Line/Orient Heights*

**B**oston doesn't have a sculpture or statue that defines it to the world in the way New York has the Statue of Liberty, Paris the Eiffel Tower, and Chicago its reflective Bean. For this historically Catholic city, though, one could do worse than an enormous Mary standing astride the world, capped with an imposing spiky crown. If only anyone knew it was here.

The humbly named Madonna Queen of the Universe Shrine in East Boston was erected in 1954 by the Don Orione Fathers, a group of Catholic priests also known as the Sons of Divine Providence. The shrine is the U.S. headquarters of the group, which is devoted to following in the footsteps of Italian Saint Luigi Orione and his service to the poor, elderly, and disabled.

The statue itself, flanked by imposing granite pillars, is composed of bronze and copper and sports a rich blue-green patina from exposure to the sea air. It is also a copy: the original stands at the Don Orione Center on Monte Mario in Rome.

In 1953, an Italian-Jewish sculptor named Arrigo Minerbi gave the 6 ton statue as a thank you gift to the Catholic community. Fleeing Nazis during World War II, Minerbi had been hidden inside the Don Orione Center. Rumor is that Minerbi crafted the first statue out of brass from pots and pans donated by Romans.

The Boston contingent requested a statue of their own, which Minerbi promptly delivered in three pieces that were reassembled stateside.

As she towers over the runways of nearby Logan Airport, Mary fittingly stands atop a globe, befitting her station as Mother of God. As such, she is a connection between our world and the next, as indicated by the positions of her hands – one pointing skyward and the other gesturing, kindly and open, toward earth. The crown – not on Mary's head but circling the full structure – underscores Mary's royal status. Before his mother, Jesus is depicted on a cross at the level of the plaza, creating a juxtaposition of the earth-bound and painful with the queenly and powerful. Still, Jesus's hands rise in triumph.

The large plaza is ringed with beautiful mosaics of the so-called "Mysteries of the Rosary," each crafted by local Italian-American artisans.

The interior of the shrine contains an intimate Marian grotto, a far more humble depiction of Mary than the Goliath outside.

# SHIP MURALS
# AT EAST BOSTON LIBRARY

*Art for the people*

*365 Bremen Street East*
*Monday–Wednesday 10am–6pm, Thursday 12pm–8pm, Friday–Saturday*
*9am–5pm*
*Blue Line/Airport*

In 1934 and 1935, a painter from Rockport, MA named Frederick Leonard King painted four grand murals with a grand title to match: "Ships Through the Ages." The lively historic paintings were created for the first library branch in East Boston, a neighborhood with close ties to the sea.

King was one of over 10,000 artists employed by the Works Progress Administration, a federal program created by President Franklin Delano Roosevelt to put Americans back to work amid surging unemployment during the Great Depression. The WPA, through its Public Works Art Project, financed the creation of paintings, theater, music, and writing and resulted in a distinctly American aesthetic, often with a focus on locally relevant subjects. There were two rules: no nudes and nothing overtly political. Tragically, many of these works have been damaged, lost, or neglected over the last 90 years.

"Ships Through the Ages" features a parade of detailed vessels and amounts to a masterclass in maritime history. King's ocean is graced by ships of all makes, from the 16th century Portuguese "Great Carrack" to Sir Francis Drake's three-mast *Golden Hind* to a colossal Cunard-White Star Liner to Robert Fulton's *Clermont*, the first commercial steamboat. From adventurers' mighty galleons to the sleek schooners of the rich and famous, King's clean lines, subtle shading, and vibrant blue waters invite close study, even for those unschooled in the nautical arts.

Several ships portrayed have a direct tie to Massachusetts: the *Flying Cloud* was built in 1851 by Donald McKay in East Boston and broke speed records; the Old New Bedford Whaler commemorates that town's place as the whaling capital of the 19th century world.

While King's paintings have survived, they are not as they were. The original Jeffries Point Branch Library closed in 1956 and the murals were cut into 20 segments, framed, and rehung. Five segments have been lost, including portrayals of the *Mayflower*, one of the first ships constructed on the Great Lakes, and a modern grain ship. Another featuring an American square-rigger sustained water damage after a fire.

A nonprofit known as the Friends of the East Boston Library has spearheaded the restoration of King's work and offers a no-questions-asked amnesty in return for the lost ships; they've even recruited a local minister to act as a go-between.

# DAVID ORTIZ JERSEY

*Red Sox legend at the airport*

*Gate C34 in Logan Airport's JetBlue Terminal*
*Blue Line/Airport*

In 2017, Gate C34 in Logan's JetBlue terminal was dedicated to Red Sox superstar David Ortiz, known locally as Big Papi. A team jersey, bearing Ortiz's signature number 34, is framed on the wall, alongside a plaque celebrating the slugger. For those boarding through the gate, the jetway is lined with photos of Ortiz in action during gameplay.

Ortiz retired in 2016 after a 20 year run in Major League Baseball. He brought the team to three World Series titles, most notably in 2004 for the first time in 86 years. Ortiz was credited for breaking the so-called "Curse of the Bambino" – the legendary punishment the Red Sox suffered for foolishly trading Babe Ruth, one of the game's all-time greats, to the New York Yankees in 1920. The Yankees went on to win more than double the championships of any competitor, and the Red Sox hit a long-lasting drought.

Ortiz is the 10th player to have his jersey number retired by the Red Sox. In a ceremony on the same day of the dedication of the Logan gate – both attended by Ortiz – a giant "34" was added to a row of other retired numbers in Fenway Stadium.

## Why fly American flags atop the jetways of the gates B-32 and C-19?

Most passengers at Logan Airport do not remember its role in the terrorist attacks of 11 September 2001, and miss the three hidden sites at the airport that memorialize this history. American Airlines Flight 11 and United Airlines Flight 175, which were hijacked and slammed into the World Trade Center towers, left from Boston. The gates used by these flights – B-32 and C-19 – fly American flags atop their jetways, viewable from windows in the terminal. No plaques describe why the flags are there, or that passengers treading the jetways are retracing the steps of the deceased.

## A memorial in honor of 9/11

In 2008, Logan did dedicate an explicit memorial in honor of 9/11 which is little visited because of its obscure location and near-ly absent mention. The memorial is a beautiful but stark glass box etched with the names of those who flew from Boston and lost their lives, along with the departure times of the respective flights – 7:59am and 8:14am. There are two winding paths leading into the memorial, each designed to mimic the flight pattern of UA 175 and AA 11 from that day.

The best way to find the memorial is to exit the airport, follow signage to the Hilton Hotel, exit through its lobby front doors, and cross the busy street ahead.

# GOLDEN STAIRS

*Steps to a new life*

*1 Ruth Street*
*Blue Line/Maverick*

The staircase at 1 Ruth Street, once burnished with brass handrails, was for thousands of immigrants their first steps into the "Land of Opportunity." They were thus called "The Golden Stairs." And today, these stairs are all that survive of the second busiest entrance into the U.S. during the first half of the 20th century; only Ellis Island saw more people pass through its doors.

From 1920 to 1954, the East Boston Immigration Station was the destination for immigrants arriving by ship who required further re-

view – those lacking documentation, those suspected of communicable diseases, criminals, the mentally ill, stowaways. About 10% of the 230,677 who came to Boston during those years ended up in the station.

The building was too small from the start. An evaluation from the office of the Surgeon General of the Public Health Service described it: "This building is of fireproof construction, one story high, and supposed to accommodate 582 aliens. The male dormitory has 35,300 cubic feet, with 272 folding bunks, affording when filled 134 cubic feet of air space per person. The female dormitory has 40,000 cubic feet, with 310 folding bunks, providing 130 cubic feet of air space per bunk."

Comforts were few; there was a fenced-in wharf on Boston Harbor for exercise. One British detainee – and eventual deportee – named Selina Chippendale recounted her experience to the *New York Times* in 1926: "I had a horrible time at the immigration station. The place was swarming with cockroaches, the food was not fit for pigs and there was no privacy. My bed consisted of two planks and I had no pillow. They call it a station, but it was more like a jail…America has a Statue of Liberty but the authorities there don't appear to know the meaning of the word."

But for those who made it through, the backstairs into East Boston were a fine reward.

Over the years, the station held notable clientele. Charles Ponzi spent a few months. Nazi operatives caught off Greenland paid a visit.

By the early 1950s, immigrants were arriving by air rather than boat, and the station closed. The property fell into disrepair. Despite its historical significance, it was torn down in 2011.

The Golden Stairs are the last vestige of this slice of immigration history in Boston. At the top, a modest park called the Golden Stairs Terrace Park provides a pleasant spot to consider the dreams of those who ascended before you.

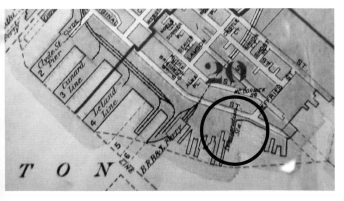

# NANTUCKET LIGHTSHIP/LV-112 MUSEUM

*A floating lighthouse*

*256 Marginal Street*
*Saturday 10am–4pm from the last Saturday in April through the last Saturday in October*
*To arrange off-season tours, email rmmjr2@comcast.net*
*Blue Line/Maverick*

*N*antucket/LV-112 is the oldest lightship in the United States, one of only 17 still in existence. Lightships functioned as floating lighthouses stationed in dangerous areas of the coasts to guide shipping traffic. The last lightship was taken out of service in 1985; they were replaced with enormous lit buoys or platforms that could withstand punishing conditions.

Active from 1936 to 1975, first as part of the U.S. Lighthouse Service and then the Coast Guard, the *Nantucket* was posted in the Nantucket Shoals, which the U.S. Lightship Museum describes as "the most remote and treacherous lighthouse station in the world" – 100 miles off the coast, anchored in 200 feet of water.

The position was exposed to extreme weather on the open ocean, out of eyesight of the mainland and far from help. Nor'easters posed particular threats, and heavy fog was common.

Aboard the *Nantucket* today, the extremes faced by the seamen stationed aboard are captured by the footprints on the bulkhead; when the ship was facing a tumultuous sea the crew would stand on the wall as the ship tipped vertically.

While the ship was equipped to be seen and heard – its foghorn can be heard 14 miles away and its light is visible from 23 miles – there were close calls and collisions. *Nantucket's* predecessor lightship was rammed by the RMS Olympic (the Titanic's sister ship) in 1934, resulting in the death of seven crew members. White Star Line, which owned the ships, financed the construction of the *Nantucket* as compensation.

At 148 feet, the *Nantucket* was the longest U.S. lightship ever built, with a double-hull and compartmentalized structure that made it virtually unsinkable. Still, two hurricanes in the 1950s battered the ship, separating its anchor chain, tearing off its rudder, smashing in portholes. In 1959, 95 mile per hour winds pushed the ship from its station. Ice on the antennas prevented communication and for four days the lightship drifted. A recovery mission located the *Nantucket* 80 miles from its station.

## "The Statue of Liberty of the Sea"

In time, the lightship became known as "The Statue of Liberty of the Sea" because it was the first sign to approaching ships that they had reached America. To get some sense of how grand that must have felt, try to time your visit to National Lighthouse Day in August, when the museum activates its light beacon and lets its foghorn roar.

# BOSTON FIRE MUSEUM

*Where Sparks fly*

*344 Congress Street*
*Saturday 10am–4pm*
*Red Line/South Station*

Dating from 1892, Boston's second oldest firehouse is home to the Boston Fire Museum, which preserves the history of the people and machinery that protect us from fires.

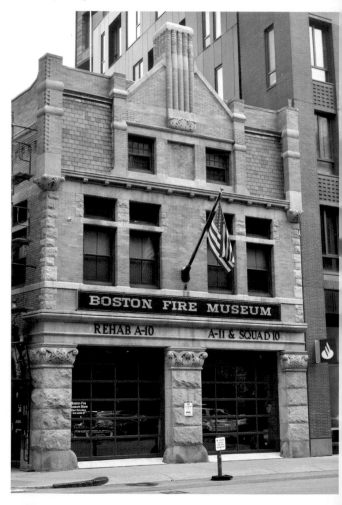

The firehouse was once home to hand- and horse-drawn fire equipment, examples of which the museum has on display. The array of implements astound. They were inventive for their times but are, by modern standards, clunky and inefficient – more Rube Goldberg than Thomas Edison.

The Thayer Boston #1 1792 Hand Tub shows just how manual the work of dousing flames once was: the cumbersome apparatus was pulled to a fire, filled with water by bucket, then pumped by hand. (It looks like a railroad handcar.) Many famous names were fire wardens in colonial Boston – Paul Revere, John Hancock, Sam Adams – and the designer of the hand tub was an apprentice to Revere.

The 1885 Washington Engine #5 hand tub required 15 men on each side to pump and, the display notes, "100 firemen to make it work effectively."

Animals were key to early firefighting efforts. The 1890 building permit notes that it had "all the appointments for a first-class stable," as well as a hayloft. (It also notes plans for a smoking room for the firefighters.) At the back of the museum, a door purports to lead to horse living quarters and from the ceiling dangles a "hanging harness" with a quick-locking collar and clips that could ready an equine in under a minute.

The rise of the automobile led to fire engines, here represented by "The Plum," a jaunty 1926 American LaFrance with an open-air driver's seat that guests can climb into.

Every inch of wall and floorspace is adorned with firefighting ephemera – badges, metals, tools, buckets, hydrants. The rafters are chockablock with retired fire helmets, and a glass cabinet is topped by a collection of antique fire helmets from around the world; Sweden's entry sports an authoritative-looking horn.

Nothing better captures the evolution of firefighting than a simple log resting amid a bevy of fire hydrants. The hollow log is in fact a piece of Boston's water main from around 1800, complete with a rough wood plug that firefighters would yank out when there was a fire.

One of the docents – members of the Boston Sparks Association (Spark refers to enthusiasts of firefighting) – noted my interest. "That's why firefighters today still call hydrants 'plugs!'"

# ANONYMOUSE INSTALLATIONS ⑨

*Mini amenities for mice*

*Five hidden locations around the city, including one at the Echeleon complex,*
*135 Seaport Boulevard*
*Red Line/South Station*

In June 2022, Boston real estate changed dramatically. Seemingly over-night, ten new buildings were erected at five unannounced locations. They each stood less than a foot high and the tenants, it would seem, were mice.

And well-cultured mice at that. They tailor their clothes at "Whiskers & Tail," with numerous bolts of fabric and various sewing accoutrements viewable through the front window. They browse classic works at the Massachusetts Museum of Fine Art. They dine out on berries and nuts at Noix de Vie (Nuts of Life), with a quick dessert from The Sugar Cube.

There is also safety infrastructure, in the form of the Mousachusetts Fire Brigade.

The teeny, highly detailed buildings were a cheeky bit of guerilla artistry by a shadowy Swedish art collective known only as AnonyMouse.

The design work is impeccable; the buildings – each scaled precisely to fit into a specific corner or opening – act as mini dioramas, complete with working interior lights. The fire brigade has a pint-sized fire engine at the ready and its neighbor, an antiquarian bookshop called Anatole's, has a handsome window display framed by intricate wood paneling.

Boston-based sleuths quickly realized that all ten installations were on properties owned by WS Development, a suspected stateside collaborator.

Indeed, AnonyMouse – whose logo is a Banksy-adjacent Mickey Mouse rip-off with a Guy Fawkes goatee – has done this before. In fact, Noix de Vie's first location was installed in Malmo, Sweden in 2016. The restaurant and its neighboring bistro "Il Topoline" (complete with a red and white awning) were an instant hit with human observers.

There is something a touch eerie in the fact that no creatures ever stir in these sets worthy of a Wes Anderson film – they never emerge to grab that copy of "Squeak" magazine or sit on the porch seats of their free-standing country home – but surely that desolation is meant to provoke. Perhaps we scared them away?

# EDWARD A. HUEBENER BRICK COLLECTION

*One brick at a time*

*195 Boston Street*
*Visit dorchesterhistoricalsociety.org for upcoming open houses and events*
*Red Line/Andrew*

The Dorchester Historical Society is home to a possibly one-of-a-kind form of folk art. Edward A. Huebener (1851–1936) was an obsessive local antiquarian and took up the habit of collecting single bricks from houses he judged significant. He then hired local artists to paint the house from which it was taken onto the collected brick. While the names of the artists are lost, the collection of over 100 bricks, housed in two cases, is both a record of their painterly skills and a valuable architectural archive.

Huebener lived at a time when Dorchester was transitioning from a rural area with larger estates to a subdivided neighborhood of Boston. (It was annexed by the city officially in 1870.) Legend has it that his proclivity for bricks stemmed from his mother's request for one to fix a slamming door. Huebener had a sharp aesthetic appreciation: by 1890, he had a shop he branded a "Hospital for Furniture," and his services included appraising antiques.

While Huebener usually waited for the demolition of a property to extend his collection, my tour guide – and president of the Dorchester Historical Society – noted that he would also occasionally simply duck into a yard and cadge a brick.

Huebener's reputation as an eccentric was well-earned: he not only made his own coffin but was rumored to occasionally sleep in it. (Upon his death, his family had him cremated.)

The bricks are handsome artworks, often with natural settings and quirky details reflecting the lives of those who dwelled in the homes. The Ward-Macondray-King House displays the beautiful gardens for which Captain Frederick William Macondray was known, as well as the Chinese pagoda he built as an observatory, likely informed by his time as a ship captain shuttling between South America and China.

The Swan House follows a design by famous architect Charles Bulfinch and emphasizes the distinctive protruding round dining room, which was 32 feet across and two stories high, with a huge domed ceiling. Colonel James Swan participated in the Boston Tea Party and fought at Bunker Hill; he entertained fellow revolutionaries, Generals Henry Knox and Lafayette, beneath that dome.

# MUSEUM OF BAD ART

*Art ... defined loosely*

*Dorchester Brewing Company*
*1250 Massachusetts Avenue*
*Sunday–Monday 11:30am–9pm, Tuesday–Thursday 11:30am–10pm,*
*Friday–Saturday 11:30am–11pm*
*Red Line or Purple Line/JFK-UMASS*

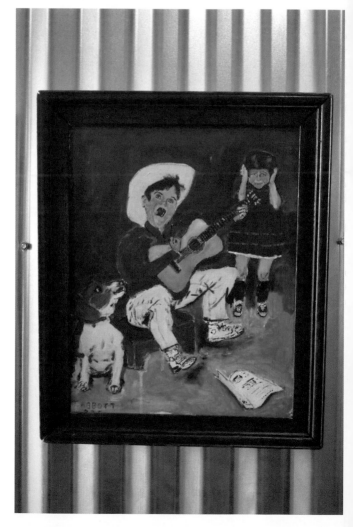

The Dorchester Brewing Company is also home to a museum collection celebrating, in its words, "Art Too Bad to Be Ignored." The Museum of Bad Art – which goes by MOBA, not to be confused with New York's MoMA – hosts rotating exhibitions from its collection of over 800 horrible artistic creations. From a surrealist nude figure astride a lobster to a painting entitled "Ferret in a Brothel" (which shows exactly that), visitors are sure to be surprised and horrified in equal measure no matter what's on display.

What makes the museum so special is that there really is a curator's eye at work: the paintings aren't just simply poorly executed or distasteful, they seem to actually aspire to give aesthetic pleasure. They wholly – and delightfully – miss the mark, of course, and that's just the intention of Curator-in-Chief Michael Frank. As the museum defines it, "what [all the works] have in common is a special quality that sets them apart in one way or another from the merely incompetent." You know it when you see it.

The museum was founded in 1993 and held its first show in the basement of a private home in March 1994. If you're lucky, you may get to see the painting that started it all, "Lucy in the Field with Flowers," an impressionistic painting featuring an older woman (who bears more than a passing resemblance to *Back to the Future*'s Doc Brown), somehow both seated and gallivanting through a beautiful field of wildflowers.

The painting – like many in the museum's archive – is by an unknown artist and was discovered in the trash. We are so much richer as a people that it was.

MOBA has ping-ponged from location to location over the years, including a residence in the basement of the historic Somerville Theater. (Basements are a theme.) Now, the museum seems well settled in the new brewing space, with ample room to hang about 40 pieces.

## Truth in captions

When you go, take the time to read the very funny descriptions of each work. They are never insulting, but nor do they shy from pointing out the obvious deficiencies. An example: "A heartening painting that makes up for lack of realism with a surplus of symbolism."

# PEAR STATUE

*A 12-foot fruit, testament to the neighborhood's farming roots*

*Edward Everett Square*
*Red Line or Purple Line/JFK-UMASS*

While gritty modern Dorchester is not known for its agricultural heritage, the 12 foot bronze pear statue standing in Everett Square is a testament to the neighborhood's history as farmland and orchards.

The statue portrays a special hybrid fruit called "the Clapp's Favorite" in honor of its inventor Thaddeus Clapp.

In the 1830s, the Clapp family's experiments with cross-breeding fruits on their extensive Dorchester plot resulted in a variety of novel fruits. The Clapp's Favorite is a hybrid of Flemish Beauty and Bartlett pears. Other experiments resulted in the pears called "Frederick Clapp" and "Sarah Clapp," but Clapp's Favorite alone has stood the test of time and is still available today.

The Clapp family's history stretches back to the early founding of America. Roger Clapp sailed from England in 1630, and the 19th century saw three Clapp brothers – Thaddeus, Frederick, and Lemuel – emerge as cutting-edge pomologists – experts in the cultivation of fruit. The area around Everett Square bears the mark of their efforts, with streets named after their experimental hybrid varieties. Keep your eyes out for the evocatively named Mayhew, Mount Vernon, Harvest, Dorset, and Bellflower Streets surrounding Everett Square.

The Clapp's Favorite pear was celebrated among the local farming community for its early ripening and mild sweetness. Thaddeus was offered $1,000 for the rights to the hybrid by the Massachusetts Agricultural Club, which planned to rename the fruit in honor of Marshall P. Wilder, a pomologist himself and agricultural activist in early Massachusetts. Thaddeus was unmoved.

The pear statue was installed in 2007 by artist Laura Baring-Gould. Note that Baring-Gould also included 10 smaller sculptures surrounding the pear, a grab bag of items representing other populations of Dorchester, including veterans (dog-tags) and Native Americans (squash, corn, beans.) She also included a triple-decker house typical of the neighborhood.

---

Near the pear statue, at 195 Boston Street, the Dorchester Historical Society is headquartered in the preserved 1806 home of William Clapp, father of Thaddeus, Frederick, and Lemuel. (see p. 268)

---

If you can't get enough of sculpted fruit, the Clapp's Favorite is also featured in bas-relief on the grave of Thaddeus Clapp in Boston's Forest Hills Cemetery. (see p. 196)

# EDWARD M. KENNEDY INSTITUTE FOR THE UNITED STATES SENATE

*Become a senator*

*210 Morrissey Boulevard*
*To arrange a visit, email info@emkinstitute.org or check hours and events at*
*emkinstitute.org*
*Red Line or Purple Line/JFK-UMASS*

Edward Kennedy, brother of President John F. Kennedy, served as a senator from Massachusetts for almost 47 years and earned the nickname "The Lion of the Senate" for his legislative prowess. He was a passionate advocate for civic engagement and believed that the general populace should understand how the U.S. Senate works to get things done. That is the mission of his institute, which sits just beside his brother's majestic Presidential Library.

The uninspiring exterior of the nonprofit hides a secret: it's not so much a museum as it is a theater. The building is essentially a box within a box. The exterior ring features educational displays and rotating exhib-

© Edward M. Kennedy Institute for the United State Senate

its but the inner gallery is the star: a full-scale replica of the U.S. Senate, sourced from a 3D survey of the actual chamber in Washington, D.C.

Visitors don't just browse the gallery – when you enter, you take on the role of a senator, right down to the assigned desk. Museum staff run simulations of Senate sessions and live floor debates on real bills, which are periodically updated to reflect issues of the day. They can range from immigration reform to climate policy to voting rights. The "senators" are encouraged to share their points of view, give speeches, respectfully argue, then cast votes on the proposed bill.

The institute also hosts re-enactments of historic debates in American history, like the decision whether or not to join the League of Nations (the progenitor of the U.N.) and the Compromise of 1850, which temporarily cooled tensions over slavery as more states were added to the country.

Visitors can also explore a re-creation of Senator Kennedy's office from the Senate's Russell Building. The walls and desk are chockablock with quirky mementos, including model ships, intimate family photos, and seascape paintings done by Kennedy himself.

Above the door is a photo of his two beloved Portuguese water dogs. So thoroughly does the office capture the senator, two tennis balls sit below the desk, ready for a visit from his canine constituents.

# FORMER KILN

## *The last vestige of an industrial marvel*

*105 Victory Road*
*Red Line/Fields Corner*

Henderson's Famous
Foot Warmer

An odd building sits just off the corner of a strip mall. One half is a two-story red-brick building with a soaring 60 foot high smokestack. The other half is a modern Early Intervention Center run by Bay Cove Human Services. The two are jarringly stitched together.

The brick building is the last vestige of an industrial marvel: the Dorchester Pottery Works.

Opened in 1895 by George Henderson, the pottery works specialized in utilitarian agricultural and industrial equipment – or as his first advertisement would have it, "Manu'r of Dip Baskets, Butter Pots, Jugs, Jars, and Flower Pots."

George also had a hit with a domestic product: the so-called "porcelain pig." The pig, also known as the "Patented Henderson Footwarmer," is a porcine ceramic bottle that could be filled with hot water and placed under the feet, including in early automobiles unequipped with sufficient heating systems.

The red-brick building was built in 1914 and contains the company's secret weapon: a circular two-story monolith "bee-hive kiln." (You can see it through the ground-floor windows.) At 22 feet across and 10.5 feet tall, the kiln is an engineering wonder. The walls are seven bricks thick, thinning out to five at the dome. Amazingly, the entire brick structure was built without mortar; the bricks are perfectly balanced, like a giant Jenga set.

The scale of the kiln allowed a month's worth of pottery to be baked at once. Once the clay was loaded in, openings in the kiln were double-bricked closed. The process from load-in to firing to cooling to load out spanned two intense weeks, with temperatures reaching 3,000 degrees Fahrenheit. One firing required 15 tons of coal and four cords of wood.

In the 1950s, the pottery works began to make tableware in a signature white and blue, with nautical and natural themes (fish, blueberries, pine cones). Through the 60s and 70s these handmade pieces became extremely popular, and eventually the on-site store had to limit customers to two purchases at a time.

If you enter the Bay Cove Human Services lobby, the receptionist will point you to a cabinet containing a number of plates, mugs, and bowls from this era.

In 1980, a fire destroyed the pottery works offices and studios, but the extraordinary kiln survived. It was built for fire.

# PEABODY SQUARE CLOCK

*Keeper of the Clock*

*Intersection of Dorchester Avenue and Ashmont Street*
*To see the clock interior and weekly winding, contact Jeff Gonyeau*
*at jeffrey.gonyeau@gmail.com*
*Red Line/Ashmont*

Installed in 1909, at 21 feet tall, with four faces, the towering clock in Peabody Square is the only architect-designed clock in Boston. It was manufactured in Roxbury by the E. Howard Clock Company. At the time, public clocks were erected by watchmakers as advertisements outside their shops. The Peabody Square Clock was the only clock erected by the city simply for the public good.

By the 1970s, the clock was badly neglected. An ill-considered plan to electrify its workings via a small motor left the clockfaces stopped at ten past one permanently. The head of the clock and its decorative details (note the four sculptures of vicious dog heads) were made of wood, and, well, time had taken its toll.

Enter the City of Boston and concerned citizens. Starting in 1999, efforts began to rebuild the head in cast iron and to de-electrify the interior.

Today the clock is powered just as it was in 1909: a pendulum in its base swings, rotates a shaft up the post, and drives a series of gears and the clocks' hands. A 132 pound weight must be hand-cranked weekly to keep the pendulum in motion.

That job falls to Jeff Gonyeau, known locally as the Keeper of the Clock. For 20 years, he has made a weekly trip to unlock the clock base, revealing its decidedly 19th century-looking mechanism. Patiently, he hand-cranks the counterweight into position, and another week can begin.

## Where does the name Peabody come from?

Peabody Square is named for Oliver Peabody and Mary Lothrop Peabody, prominent Bostonians of the 1800s. On 28 December 1879, the Unitarian couple set out by carriage to attend services at King's Chapel in Boston. A snowstorm made the drive impossible, and their driver suggested they take shelter at All Saints, an Episcopalian church. It was the Feast of the Holy Innocents, which commemorates the killing of children by King Herod, who feared the birth of Jesus. For the Peabodys, the holy day was particularly poignant, as their young daughter had recently died. They were so moved by the sermon of All Saints's rector, they converted to the Episcopalian faith, became patrons of All Saints, and financed the building of the massive stone edifice that anchors Peabody Square today.

# ABANDONED BEAR ENCLOSURES ⓰

## *A forgotten zoo*

*Franklin Park Playstead Road*
*Orange Line/Jackson Square*

In a remote area of a modern-day city park sit the ruins of a zoo. Four bear enclosures have been left to rot away for 50 years, and while the accommodations for the bears were meager – trees and shallow swimming pools, surrounded by intimidating metal fences – there was a single piece of decoration that miraculously remains intact: embedded in the wall of one of the cages is a beautiful relief sculpture of two mighty bears on their hind legs, proudly holding aloft the 1912 seal of the City of Boston.

Today, Franklin Park is not one of Boston's well-known greenspaces, even though it clocks in at 527 acres and was laid out by famed landscape architect Frederick Law Olmsted. Olmsted's intention was for this park to be a pastoral escape from the city. He was opposed to zoos in his parks, believing they were too expensive and visually disruptive to his curated bucolic scenes.

Nevertheless, following Olmsted's death in 1903, Boston Metropolitan Parks Commission Superintendent John Pettigrew advocated for a free zoo in the park to attract more visitors. Landscape architect Arthur Shurtleff designed the zoo according to the direction of the commission, which insisted on both indigenous and exotic animals. And so the bear dens were opened in the autumn of 1912: cage one for grizzlies, two and three for black bears, and four for polar bears.

The first residents were purchased from Yellowstone National Park and Germany. Walking through the overgrown enclosures today, the iron bars, cold concrete floors, and small pools may seem cruel, but they met the standards of the time. Crowds flocked to the zoo in the early years, with a record-breaking 20 million visitors in 1920. The Depression and World War II, though, strained the zoo's finances.

On 28 January 1945, the *New York Times* recounted a Boston City Councillor's "proposal to shoot the animals at popular Franklin Park Zoo and use the maintenance money for playground development... [The Councillor] had suggested that the animals' food allotment – $23,500 a year – be turned over to the Park Commission and the dead animals used as fertilizer." Outraged local children created a "Save the Animals" club and won the day, though visitation remained low.

The 1950s to the 1970s saw many proposals for improvements to the park, but the bear enclosures were remote from the core exhibits and sank into disrepair. In 1970, the dens were closed for good, and the bears were sold off to various zoos.

# MATTAPAN TROLLEY

*Ride in a time capsule*

*500 River Street*
*Red Line/Ashmont*

I n 1944-45, the Boston transit system got an upgrade: the introduction of a fleet of trolley cars called PCCs, which stands for "Presidential Conference Committee." The PCC consisted of industry insiders, manufacturers and transit leaders who got together in the 1930s to design a new, improved, reliable, and comfortable streetcar that Americans who were tempted by automobiles might fall in love with. The result was the PCCs, which were shipped across the world, from Toronto to Mexico City, Los Angeles to Brooklyn. Boston was home to 346 PCCs.

The *Boston Globe* noted some of the PCCs' advanced safety features with admiration right from the start: "The pedal on the left is known as 'the dead man's brake.' Before the car can be operated, this pedal must be pressed down. Theoretically, if the operator collapses, the pressure of his foot on the pedal is lifted and the car is braked to a stop automatically." The *Globe* also wondered at "[s]eventeen switches in a line in front of the

© MBTA

operator [that] control power shutoff, lights, doors, heat, sand, and gong." Indeed, the cars proved shockingly hardy, many going on to be resold to other transit systems or gracing roads and rails into the 1980s. The PCCs were popular with the public from the start, not least because they significantly cut down noise by employing generous amounts of rubber around anything that vibrated, rattled, or shook.

They were also handsome – the Boston cars sported a mellow orange and cream paint job, with a single headlight bordered by Art Deco chrome wings.

Those chrome wings continue to fly to this day on the 2.6 mile "Mattapan-Ashmont high-speed line," making it one of the last PCC lines in the U.S., and the only line to have never stopped using the cars. "Highspeed," of course, is relative: the name refers to the fact that only two city streets interrupt its path. The PCCs – currently 10 remain in the fleet – trundle from Dorchester to Mattapan in 10 minutes, straight through the Cedar Grove Cemetery.

If you are able to peek at the operator's dashboard, note that the same line of toggles remains, including a "Sand" switch, which used to release sand onto the tracks to improve traction in slippery New England winter conditions.

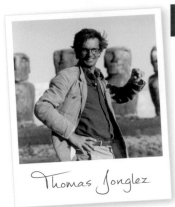

*Thomas Jonglez*

It was September 1995 and Thomas Jonglez was in Peshawar, the northern Pakistani city 20 kilometres from the tribal zone he was to visit a few days later. It occurred to him that he should record the hidden aspects of his native city, Paris, which he knew so well. During his seven-month trip back home from Beijing, the countries he crossed took in Tibet (entering clandestinely, hidden under blankets in an overnight bus), Iran and Kurdistan. He never took a plane but travelled by boat, train or bus, hitchhiking, cycling, on horseback or on foot, reaching Paris just in time to celebrate Christmas with the family.

On his return, he spent two fantastic years wandering the streets of the capital to gather material for his first "secret guide", written with a friend. For the next seven years he worked in the steel industry until the passion for discovery overtook him. He launched Jonglez Publishing in 2003 and moved to Venice three years later.

In 2013, in search of new adventures, the family left Venice and spent six months travelling to Brazil, via North Korea, Micronesia, the Solomon Islands, Easter Island, Peru and Bolivia.

After seven years in Rio de Janeiro, he now lives in Berlin with his wife and three children.

Jonglez Publishing produces a range of titles in nine languages, released in 40 countries.

## ACKNOWLEDGEMENTS

Endless thanks to my wife and favorite travel partner Katherine Mackey, whose support and patience made "Secret Boston" possible. Thanks to Charlie and Penelope, with whom I hope to revisit these sites in the years to come. Many thanks to Ria Samaroo, for the gift of time. Thank you to Jane Schmitt for your tireless encouragement and love. Thank you to Cindy Mackey for sharing many invaluable insights as the book came together.

Thank you to Brendan, Ryan, and Rob Schmitt and Chris Mackey for pepping me up when writing seemed daunting. Thank you to Emily Mackey for the years-long loan of your camera.

Thank you to Ryan Davis, the cohost on "Out of Office: A Travel Podcast" and a great lover of Boston.

Thanks to Ann and Donovan Moore, both inspirations. Thanks to my cavalcade of professional mentors and influences, not least Jon Steel, Nathaniel Nickerson, Greg Morgan, Ayr Muir, Mitchell Weiss, and Grant Schneider. Thank you to Betty and Tom Hayden, such essential friends.

Thank you to Rick Steves, who opened the world to me through his guidebooks.

A special note of gratitude to Thomas Jonglez, Clémence Mathé, and all the staff of Jonglez Publishing. The "Secret" series has inspired my travel for years; your curiosity is infectious.

This book is dedicated to the memories of my father Bob Schmitt and my father-in-law Bill Mackey.

**Maps:** Cyrille Suss – **Layout:** Emmanuelle Willard Toulemonde – **Copy-editing:** Sue Pollack – **Proofreading:** Lee Dickinson – **Publishing:** Clémence Mathé

© JONGLEZ 2024
Registration of copyright: June 2024 – Edition: 01
ISBN: 978-2-36195-717-9
Printed in Bulgaria by Dedrax